2018 SQA Specimen and Past Papers with Answers

Higher
GRAPHIC COMMUNICATION

2017 & 2018 Exams
and 2018 Specimen Question Paper

Hodder Gibson Study Skills Advice – Higher Graphic Communication	– page 3
Hodder Gibson Study Skills Advice – General	– page 5
2017 EXAM	– page 7
2018 EXAM	– page 37
2018 SPECIMEN QUESTION PAPER (FOR 2019 EXAM)	– page 69
ANSWERS	– page 101

This book contains the official SQA 2017 and 2018 Exams, and the 2018 Specimen Question Paper for Higher Graphic Communication, with associated SQA-approved answers modified from the official marking instructions that accompany the paper.

In addition the book contains study skills advice. This advice has been specially commissioned by Hodder Gibson, and has been written by experienced senior teachers and examiners in line with the Higher syllabus and assessment outlines. This is not SQA material but has been devised to provide further guidance for Higher examinations.

Hodder Gibson is grateful to the copyright holders for permission to use their material. Every effort has been made to trace the copyright holders and to obtain their permission for the use of copyright material. Hodder Gibson will be happy to receive information allowing us to rectify any error or omission in future editions.

Permission has been sought from all relevant copyright holders and Hodder Gibson is grateful for the use of the following:

Image © Nikonaft/Shutterstock.com (2017 page 10);
Image © marina_ua/Shutterstock.com (2017 page 10);
Image © 13Imagery/Shutterstock.com (2017 page 12);
Image © Irina Bg/Shutterstock.com (2017 page 12);
Image © ORLIO/Shutterstock.com (2017 page 12);
Image © Casey K. Bishop/Shutterstock.com (2017 page 12);
Image © legaa/stock.adobe.com (2017 page 12);
Image © one AND only/Shutterstock.com (2017 page 12);
Two images © EugeneOnischenko/Shutterstock.com (2017 pages 14 & 16);
Image © EPSTOCK/Shutterstock.com (2018 page 12);
Image © Wanzer/Shutterstock.com (2018 page 12);
Three images © alexandre zveiger/stock.adobe.com (2018 page 12);
Image © ESB Professional/Shutterstock.com (2018 Supplementary Sheet page page 5);
Image © Robert Kneschke/Shutterstock.com (2018 Supplementary Sheet page 5);
Image © grmarc/Shutterstock.com (2018 Supplementary Sheet page 5);
Image © Santi S/Shutterstock.com (2018 Supplementary Sheet page 5);
The logo for Ray-Ban © Luxottica Group S.p.A. (2018 SQP page 9, 11, 12, 14);
Image © Rhea Bue (Shades of Style) (2018 SQP page 9, 12, 14);
Two images © Nicoll Russell Studios (2018 SQP page 15);
Three images of the Glasgow Riverside Museum of Transport. Reproduced by permission of Zaha Hadid Architects (2018 SQP page 25).

Hachette UK's policy is to use papers that are natural, renewable and recyclable products and made from wood grown in sustainable forests. The logging and manufacturing processes are expected to conform to the environmental regulations of the country of origin.

Orders: please contact Bookpoint Ltd, 130 Park Drive, Milton Park, Abingdon, Oxon OX14 4SE. Telephone: (44) 01235 827827. Fax: (44) 01235 400454. Lines are open 9.00–5.00, Monday to Saturday, with a 24-hour message answering service. Visit our website at www.hoddereducation.co.uk. Hodder Gibson can also be contacted directly at hoddergibson@hodder.co.uk

This collection first published in 2018 by
Hodder Gibson, an imprint of Hodder Education,
An Hachette UK Company
211 St Vincent Street
Glasgow G2 5QY

Higher 2017 and 2018 Exam Papers and Answers; 2018 Specimen Question Paper and Answers © Scottish Qualifications Authority. Study Skills section © Hodder Gibson. All rights reserved. Apart from any use permitted under UK copyright law, no part of this publication may be reproduced or transmitted in any form or by any means, electronic or mechanical, including photocopying and recording, or held within any information storage and retrieval system, without permission in writing from the publisher or under licence from the Copyright Licensing Agency Limited. Further details of such licences (for reprographic reproduction) may be obtained from the Copyright Licensing Agency Limited, www.cla.co.uk

Typeset by Aptara, Inc.

Printed in the Spain

A catalogue record for this title is available from the British Library

ISBN: 978-1-5104-5673-0

2 1

2019 2018

Introduction

Higher Graphic Communication

This book of SQA past papers contains the question papers used in the 2017 and 2018 exams (with the answers at the back of the book). A specimen question paper reflecting the requirements, content and duration of the revised exam from 2019 is also included. All of the question papers included in the book provide excellent, representative practice for the final exams.

Using the 2017 and 2018 past papers as part of your revision will help you to develop the vital skills and techniques needed for the exam, and will help you to identify any knowledge gaps you may have.

It is always a very good idea to refer to SQA's website for the most up-to-date course specification documents. Further details can be found in the Higher Graphic Communication section on the SQA website: www.sqa.org.uk/sqa/47929.html

The course

The aims of the course are to enable you to understand how graphic communication is used every day in industry and society and to develop skills and techniques used in creating graphics to suit a range of functions and purposes.

The types of graphics you will learn about include:

- **preliminary** design graphics
- technical **production** drawings
- high-impact **promotional** graphics.

These are known as the **3Ps**. Your coursework projects and exam questions are based on these three types of graphic as well as the impact on society and the environment of producing these graphics. The knowledge you need for the exam will come from the work you do during your coursework tasks and the skills you develop during the course.

How you are assessed and graded

Course Assessment

The grade for the Higher course is derived from two course assessments:

- **The assignment**

This is the project you will complete in February and March. It has an 8-hour time limit and it is worth **50 marks**. Your assignment will be conducted under supervised conditions and represents 36% of the course assessment.

- **The exam paper**

The course exam paper is worth **90 marks**. The exam will be conducted under supervised conditions and represents 64% of the course assessment.

The total, 140 marks, is graded from A to D for a pass.

The exam

The exam is **two hours and thirty minutes** long and is worth a total of **90 marks**. It will include a mix of short questions and more extended questions relating to preliminary, production and promotional graphics. There will be different types of graphic to interpret before questions can be answered. These graphics can be complex and detailed and it would be a mistake to jump straight in with answers. It is vital to spend time studying the graphics and annotations first.

Look at the marks awarded for each question. This is a good indicator of the length of answer you should give. For example, a 3-mark question will need you to make three distinct points, while a 1-mark question may require only a single point. Each mark should take around 1½ minutes to earn with some reading time left over, so plan your time accordingly.

Sketching

Exam questions will be set so that you can answer in writing. However, some questions will invite you to answer using annotated sketches or drawings and space will be left so that you may sketch your answer. **Always take this opportunity.**

Remember:

- It is easier and quicker to describe your answer graphically with annotations.
- This is an exam about graphics and you have all the graphic skills you need.
- The quality of your sketching will not be assessed but the clarity of your answer is important, so make the sketches and annotations clear and detailed.
- Plan your sketches in a light pencil and firm in with a black pen.

Answering 3D CAD modelling questions

You should always:

- study the model and any other sketches, drawings or notes.
- identify what modelling techniques have been used (extrude, revolve, loft, helices or extrude along a path).

- describe the steps such as: new sketch, draw profile, select axis and revolve, etc.
- include reference to the dimensions provided.
- describe any additional edits used: array, subtract, shell, etc.
- importantly, make sketches to help describe the steps.
- ensure your sketches are firmed in and outlined in pen to enable scanning of your answers.

Answering creative layout questions

These questions will ask you to identify how DTP features and design elements and principles have been used in a layout. You are likely to be asked to explain how the use of these features improves the layout.
You should always:

- study the layout: don't rush this; every item in the layout has a purpose, so take time to work out what these are.
- identify the DTP features or design elements and principles used.
- think carefully about the role each item has in the layout: does it add contrast, create harmony, suggest depth, develop a dominant focal point, unify the layout, create emphasis or connect or separate parts? The feature you are asked about will do one or more of these things. Your task is to spot which, and explain how.

Skills and knowledge

The skills and knowledge the exam will test are:

Problem solving: explain how you would model, render or assemble a 3D CAD model or create a 2D CAD drawing.

Creative skills: describe how the graphic designer used design elements and principles to create an effective layout.

DTP features and edits: explain how the graphic designer used Desktop Publishing features to achieve an effective layout or how you might use DTP features to improve a poor layout.

Advantages and disadvantages: justify the best methods to choose when creating graphics, e.g. describe the advantages of modelling a new product using 3D CAD.

Knowledge of drawing standards: explain how drawing standards should be applied to complex production drawings including technical detail.

Spatial awareness: testing your ability to interpret and understand drawings.

Graphics in society: explain how graphics are used, and the impact graphics have, in our society.

Graphics and the environment: explain how we can create and use graphics without damaging our fragile environment.

At the end of the exam, check over your answers and read the questions again. Double-check that you have answered the question you have been asked. You should have plenty of time.

Practising the type of questions you are likely to face in the Higher exam is vital. This book will give you experience of the problem solving, CAD, creative layout and knowledge questions you will face in the exam. Ensure you tackle these important sections before your prelim and final course exam.

Good luck!

Remember that the rewards for passing Higher Graphic Communication are well worth it! Your pass will help you get the future you want for yourself. In the exam, be confident in your own ability. If you're not sure how to answer a question, trust your instincts and just give it a go anyway – keep calm and don't panic! GOOD LUCK!

Study Skills – what you need to know to pass exams!

General exam revision: 20 top tips

When preparing for exams, it is easy to feel unsure of where to start or how to revise. This guide to general exam revision provides a good starting place, and, as these are very general tips, they can be applied to all your exams.

1. Start revising in good time.

Don't leave revision until the last minute – this will make you panic and it will be difficult to learn. Make a revision timetable that counts down the weeks to go.

2. Work to a study plan.

Set up sessions of work spread through the weeks ahead. Make sure each session has a focus and a clear purpose. What will you study, when and why? Be realistic about what you can achieve in each session, and don't be afraid to adjust your plans as needed.

3. Make sure you know exactly when your exams are.

Get your exam dates from the SQA website and use the timetable builder tool to create your own exam schedule. You will also get a personalised timetable from your school, but this might not be until close to the exam period.

4. Make sure that you know the topics that make up each course.

Studying is easier if material is in manageable chunks – why not use the SQA topic headings or create your own from your class notes? Ask your teacher for help on this if you are not sure.

5. Break the chunks up into even smaller bits.

The small chunks should be easier to cope with. Remember that they fit together to make larger ideas. Even the process of chunking down will help!

6. Ask yourself these key questions for each course:

- Are all topics compulsory or are there choices?
- Which topics seem to come up time and time again?
- Which topics are your strongest and which are your weakest?

Use your answers to these questions to work out how much time you will need to spend revising each topic.

7. Make sure you know what to expect in the exam.

The subject-specific introduction to this book will help with this. Make sure you can answer these questions:

- How is the paper structured?
- How much time is there for each part of the exam?
- What types of question are involved? These will vary depending on the subject so read the subject-specific section carefully.

8. Past papers are a vital revision tool!

Use past papers to support your revision wherever possible. This book contains the answers and mark schemes too – refer to these carefully when checking your work. Using the mark scheme is useful; even if you don't manage to get all the marks available first time when you first practise, it helps you identify how to extend and develop your answers to get more marks next time – and of course, in the real exam.

9. Use study methods that work well for you.

People study and learn in different ways. Reading and looking at diagrams suits some students. Others prefer to listen and hear material – what about reading out loud or getting a friend or family member to do this for you? You could also record and play back material.

10. There are three tried and tested ways to make material stick in your long-term memory:

- Practising – e.g. rehearsal, repeating
- Organising – e.g. making drawings, lists, diagrams, tables, memory aids
- Elaborating – e.g. incorporating the material into a story or an imagined journey

11. Learn actively.

Most people prefer to learn actively – for example, making notes, highlighting, redrawing and redrafting, making up memory aids, or writing past paper answers. A good way to stay engaged and inspired is to mix and match these methods – find the combination that best suits you. This is likely to vary depending on the topic or subject.

12. Be an expert.

Be sure to have a few areas in which you feel you are an expert. This often works because at least some of them will come up, which can boost confidence.

13. Try some visual methods.

Use symbols, diagrams, charts, flashcards, post-it notes etc. Don't forget – the brain takes in chunked images more easily than loads of text.

14. Remember – practice makes perfect.

Work on difficult areas again and again. Look and read – then test yourself. You cannot do this too much.

15. Try past papers against the clock.

Practise writing answers in a set time. This is a good habit from the start but is especially important when you get closer to exam time.

16. Collaborate with friends.

Test each other and talk about the material – this can really help. Two brains are better than one! It is amazing how talking about a problem can help you solve it.

17. Know your weaknesses.

Ask your teacher for help to identify what you don't know. Try to do this as early as possible. If you are having trouble, it is probably with a difficult topic, so your teacher will already be aware of this – most students will find it tough.

18. Have your materials organised and ready.

Know what is needed for each exam:
- Do you need a calculator or a ruler?
- Should you have pencils as well as pens?
- Will you need water or paper tissues?

19. Make full use of school resources.

Find out what support is on offer:
- Are there study classes available?
- When is the library open?
- When is the best time to ask for extra help?
- Can you borrow textbooks, study guides, past papers, etc.?
- Is school open for Easter revision?

20. Keep fit and healthy!

Try to stick to a routine as much as possible, including with sleep. If you are tired, sluggish or dehydrated, it is difficult to see how concentration is even possible. Combine study with relaxation, drink plenty of water, eat sensibly, and get fresh air and exercise – all these things will help more than you could imagine. Good luck!

HIGHER
2017

FOR OFFICIAL USE

H

National Qualifications 2017

Mark

X735/76/01

Graphic Communication

WEDNESDAY, 10 MAY
1:00 PM – 3:00 PM

Fill in these boxes and read what is printed below.

Full name of centre

Town

Forename(s)

Surname

Number of seat

Date of birth
Day   Month   Year   Scottish candidate number

Total marks — 70

Attempt ALL questions.

All dimensions are in mm.

All technical sketches and drawings use third angle projection.

You may use rulers, compasses or trammels for measuring.

In all questions you may use sketches and annotations to support your answer if you wish.

Write your answers clearly in the spaces provided in this booklet. Additional space for answers is provided at the end of this booklet. If you use this space you must clearly identify the question number you are attempting.

Use **blue** or **black** ink.

Before leaving the examination room you must give this booklet to the Invigilator; if you do not, you may lose all the marks for this paper.

SQA

Total marks — 70

Attempt ALL questions

1. A CAD technician created a 3D model of the bicycle, shown below.

   (a) (i) Describe, giving two reasons, how a 3D CAD model can be used to aid production. **2**

   (ii) Describe, giving two reasons, how the 3D CAD model can be used to support manufacture through testing. **2**

1. (continued)

   (b) A new brake disc design was requested for the bicycle.

   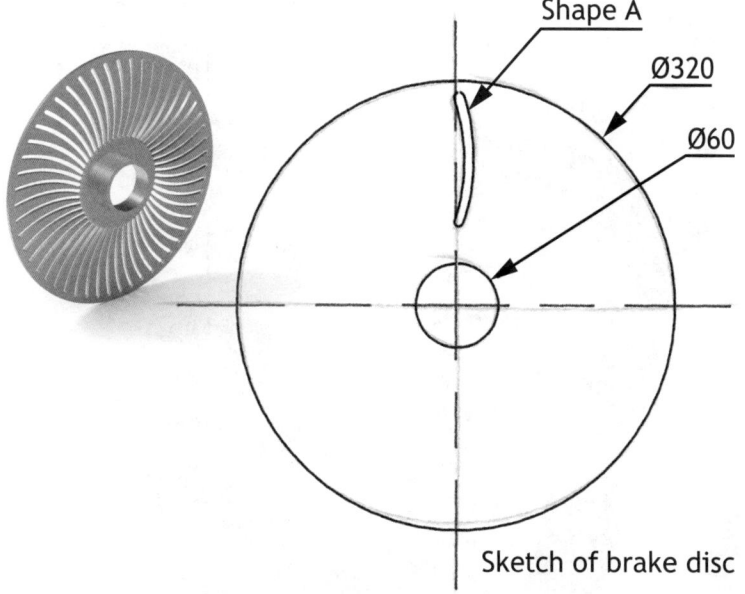

   Sketch of brake disc

   Shape A was to be repeated 60 times. State the CAD edit that would be used to create the feature.

   1

   [Turn over

1. (continued)

   (c) The bicycle uses a spring as part of the suspension system, shown below.

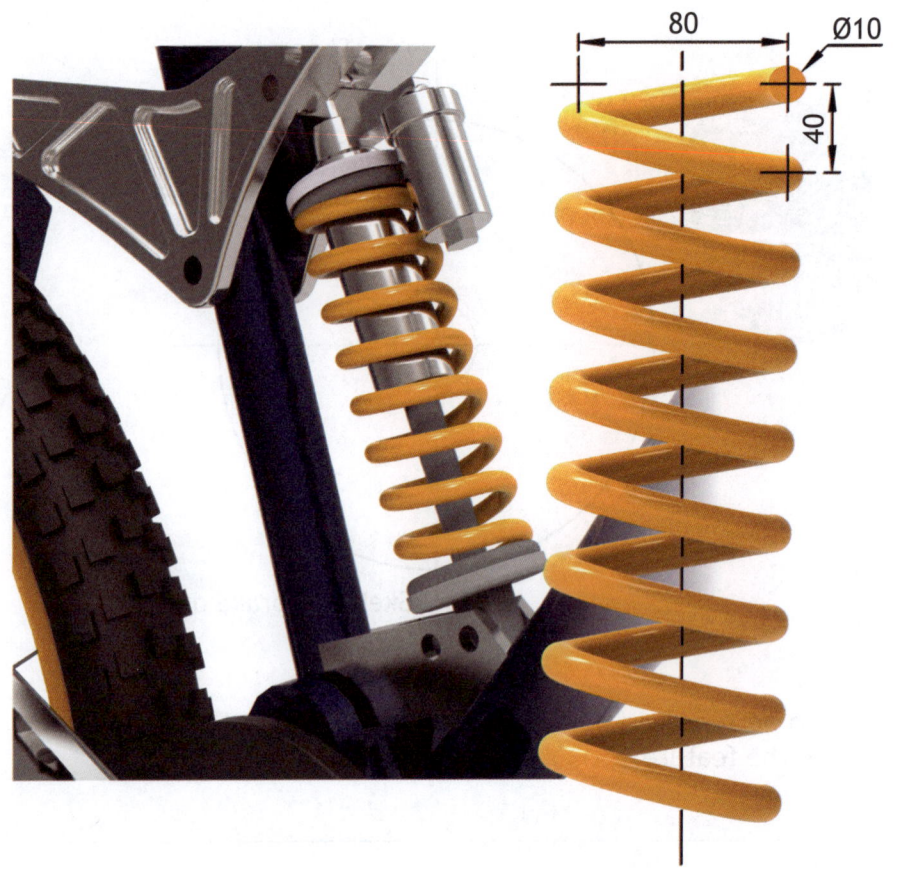

   The spring was modelled as a separate component using 3D CAD.

   Describe the 3D CAD technique used to model the spring.

   You must make reference to the dimensions above.

   You may use sketches to illustrate your answer.

   3

1. (continued)

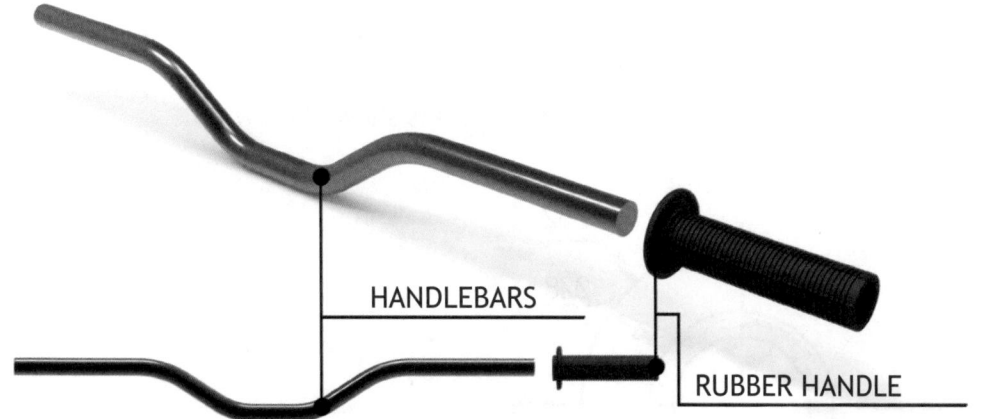

(d) The handlebars were 3D CAD modelled as a single component.

Describe the modelling technique used to generate the component. 2

You may use sketches to illustrate your answer.

Rubber handles were required to cover the handlebars.

The CAD technician used top down modelling to create the rubber handles.

(e) Describe two advantages of **top down modelling** in relation to these components. 2

MARKS | DO NOT WRITE IN THIS MARGIN

1. (continued)

(f) The shape of the rubber handle was sketched prior to being modelled using 3D CAD.

The orthographic sketch of the rubber handle is shown below.

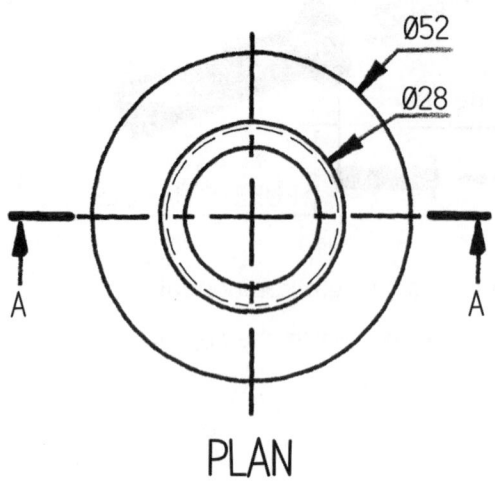

Ø52
Ø28
A
A
PLAN
4
B
130
5
5
SECTION A–A
Grips repeated 38 times
With a 2mm gap
5
□1
Partial Enlarged View B
Handle Sketch
All sizes in mm
Not to scale

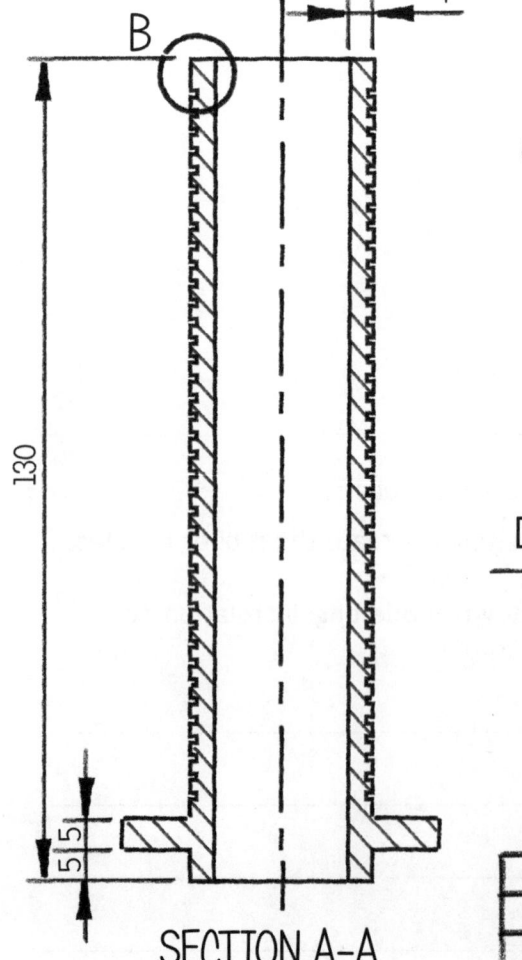

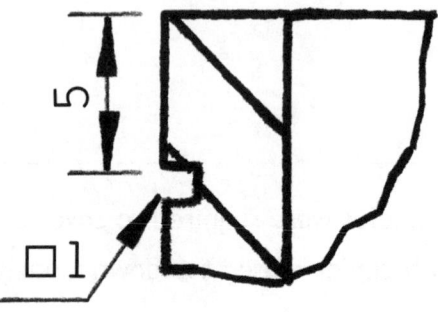

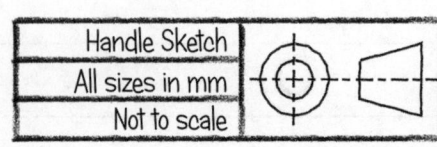

MARKS | DO NOT WRITE IN THIS MARGIN

1. (f) (continued)

Describe the 3D CAD technique used to model the rubber handle with reference to the dimensions in the sketch of the handle (shown opposite). 6

You may use sketches to illustrate your answer.

[Turn over

1. (continued)

   (g) Two sectional views of the bicycle crank are shown below.

   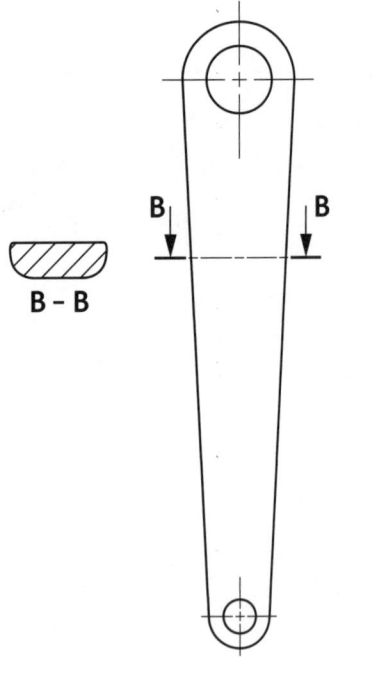

   Figure 1

   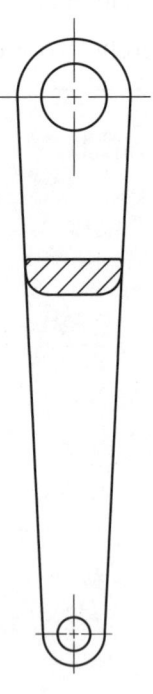

   Figure 2

   (i) State the type of sectional view shown in Figure 1.   1

   _____

   (ii) State the type of sectional view shown in Figure 2.   1

   _____

[Turn over for next question

DO NOT WRITE ON THIS PAGE

2. Graphics 1 and 2 are both used within the building industry and serve different purposes.

Graphic 1

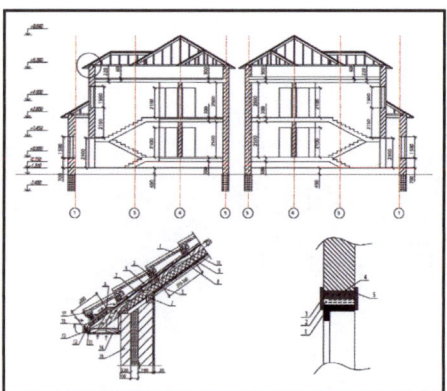

Graphic 2

(a) State the intended user and explain the purpose of each graphic.

(i) Graphic 1   2

User _____

Purpose _____

_____

_____

(ii) Graphic 2   2

User _____

Purpose _____

_____

_____

2. **(continued)**

   (b) A construction company uses CAD software that makes use of **cloud computing**. The company engineers visit construction sites on a regular basis and require access to the most current CAD data.

   (i) Describe two advantages that **cloud computing** can offer the construction company. **2**

   _____

   _____

   _____

   _____

   (ii) Describe two disadvantages of **cloud storage**. **2**

   _____

   _____

   _____

   _____

   [Turn over

3. A layout from a health magazine is shown below.

(a) The graphic designer has used **emphasis** in the layout shown above.

Describe how each of these items has been emphasised.

(i) The pull quote.

_____

_____

(ii) The body text.

_____

_____

(iii) The photograph of the model.

_____

_____

3. (continued)

(b) Explain, giving two reasons, why the graphic designer has limited the use of colour in the layout. **2**

(c) Describe the effect of using both serif **and** sans serif fonts in this layout. **1**

(d) The title is in a serif typeface which the graphic designer felt was suitable for use in the layout.

Explain why this is a suitable typeface for this layout. **1**

(e) Describe how the graphic designer has created **rhythm** in the layout. **1**

(f) Describe how the graphic designer has created **texture** in the layout. **1**

(g) Describe how the graphic designer has used **value** in the layout. **1**

[Turn over

4. A graphic designer for a sports magazine created Layout 1 as a draft idea for a basketball article.

The magazine editor suggested DTP features to create better visual impact.

The graphic designer then produced a second draft, Layout 2.

Layout 1

Layout 2

4. (continued)

   (a) Identify four additional DTP features that have been added to Layout 2 and explain, giving two reasons for each, how they improve the layout.

   (i) (A) Feature _____ 1

       (B) Reasons _____ 2
       _____
       _____
       _____

   (ii) (A) Feature _____ 1

        (B) Reasons _____ 2
        _____
        _____
        _____

   (iii) (A) Feature _____ 1

         (B) Reasons _____ 2
         _____
         _____
         _____

   (iv) (A) Feature _____ 1

        (B) Reasons _____ 2
        _____
        _____
        _____

[Turn over

4. (continued)

   (b) High-resolution images used in the magazine were downloaded from a photo stock website for a small cost.

   (i) Explain what is meant by the term high-resolution.

   (ii) State the name of a suitable file type for an image.

   (c) Prior to paying for the high-resolution images, low-resolution samples were available to download for free. These images contained watermarks, as shown above.

   Explain, giving two reasons, why watermarks are added to the free images.

[Turn over for next question

DO NOT WRITE ON THIS PAGE

5. A packaging proposal is shown below.

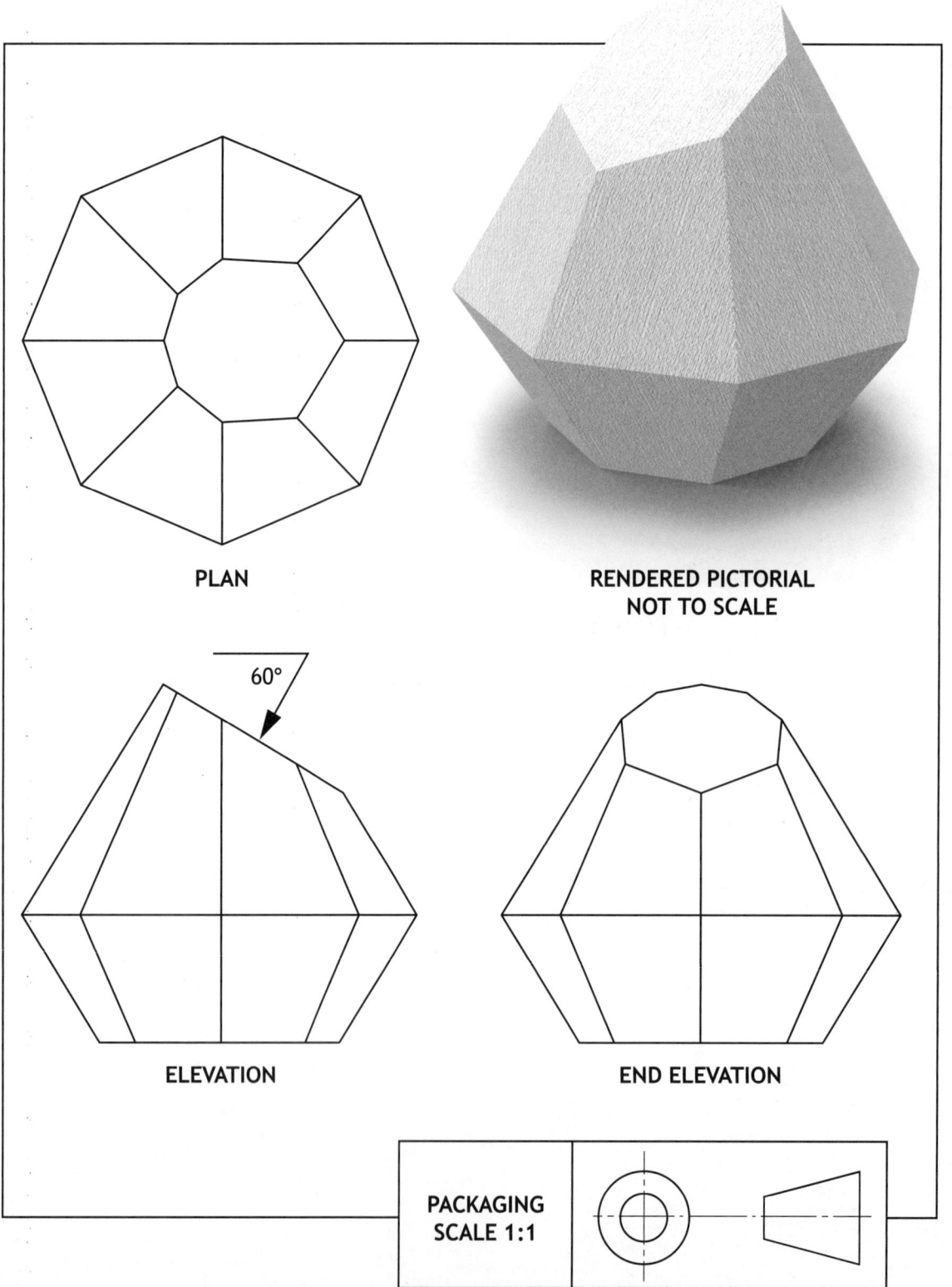

5. (continued)

   (a) Indicate the correct **auxiliary view** by ticking (✓) a box below.   1
   Use a ruler, trammel or compasses to measure.

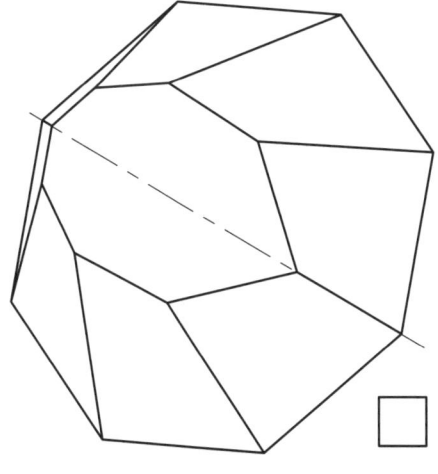

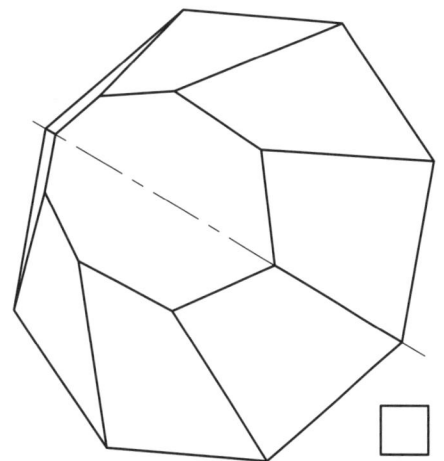

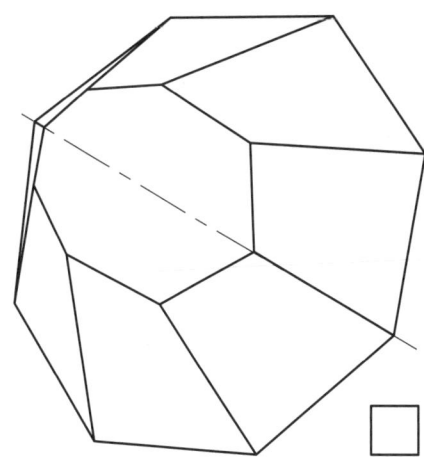

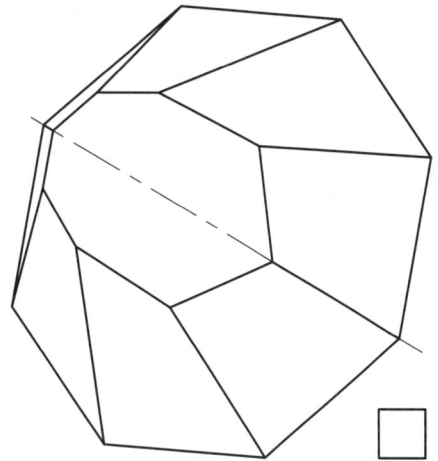

[Turn over

5. (continued)

(b) The orthographic drawing of the packaging is shown below. The packaging will have different information on various faces.

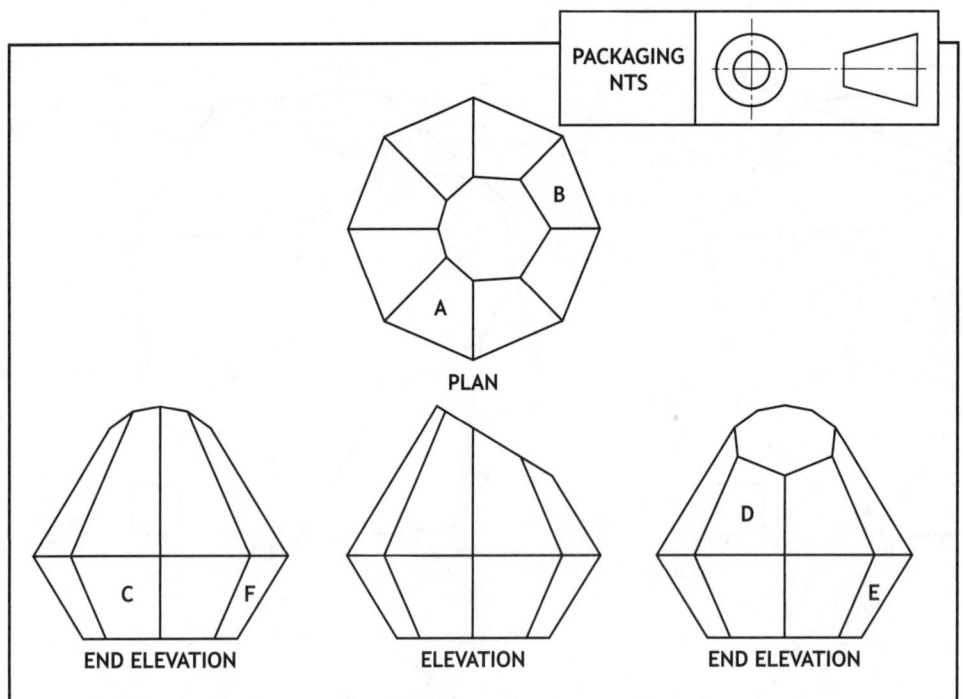

Indicate the position of faces A–F on the surface development below. The surface development is shown from the **outside**.

6

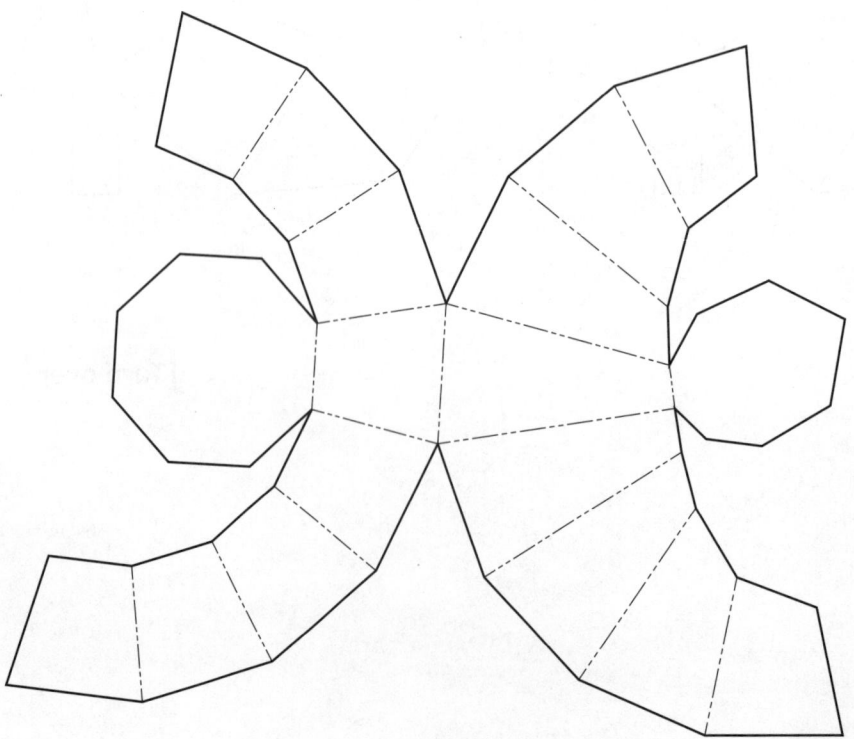

6. A CAD technician created a 3D model and technical drawing of an oil pump.

Use the exploded view and parts list on the **Supplementary Sheet for use with Question 6**, provided, to answer this question.

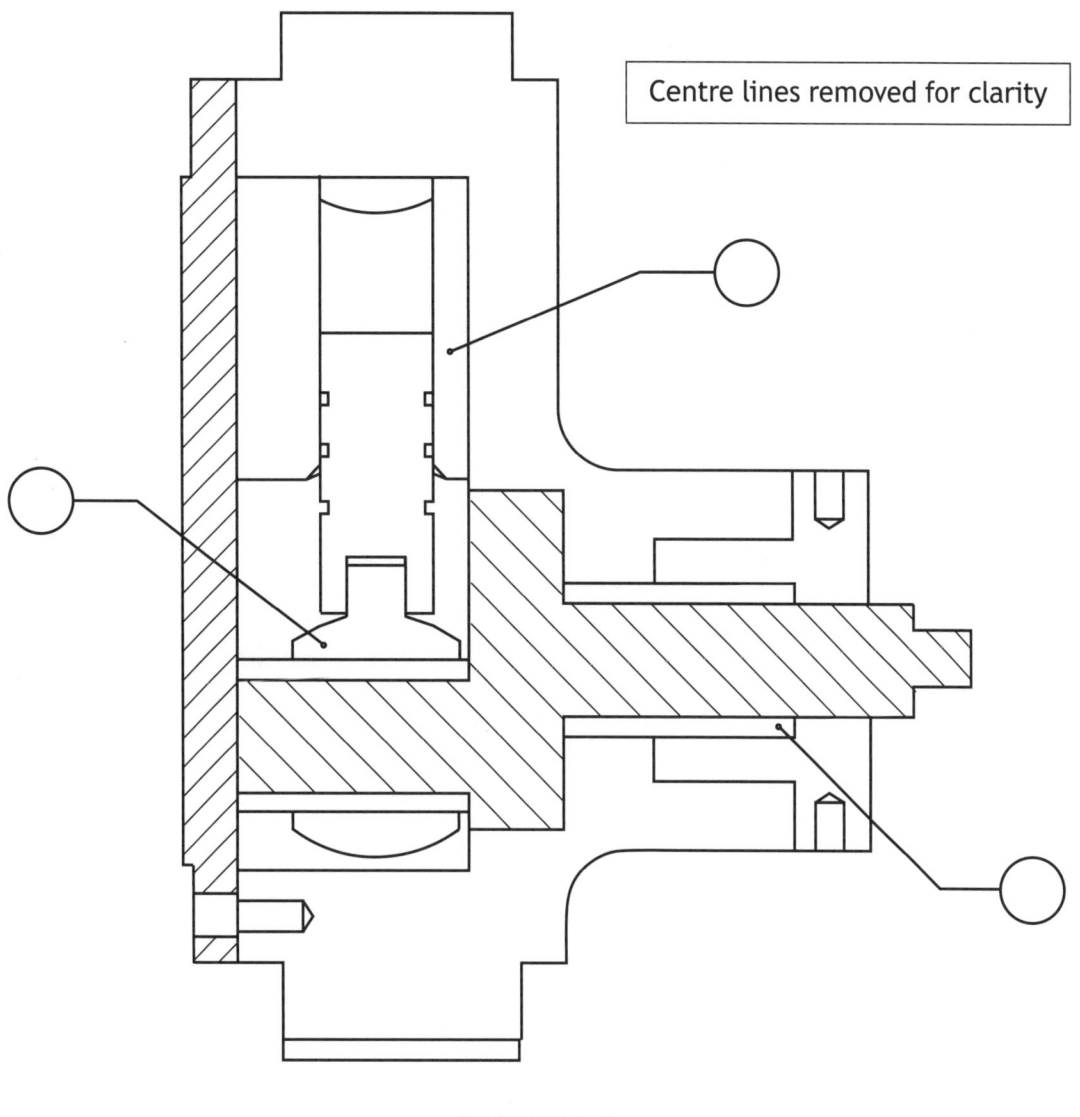

SECTION A-A

(a) Complete Section A-A above by applying hatching lines to appropriate areas in accordance to British Standard conventions. **6**

(b) Add the part number of the three components indicated on Section A-A above. **3**

[END OF QUESTION PAPER]

ADDITIONAL SPACE FOR ANSWERS

ADDITIONAL SPACE FOR ANSWERS

National Qualifications 2017

X735/76/11

Graphic Communication Supplementary Sheet

WEDNESDAY, 10 MAY
1:00 PM — 3:00 PM

Supplementary Sheet for use with Question 6.

Supplementary Sheet for use with Question 6

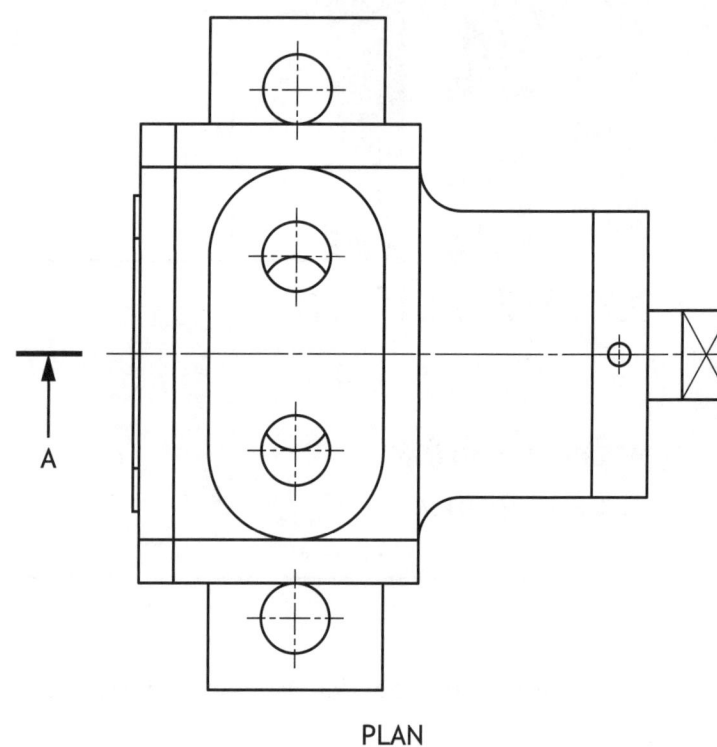

PLAN

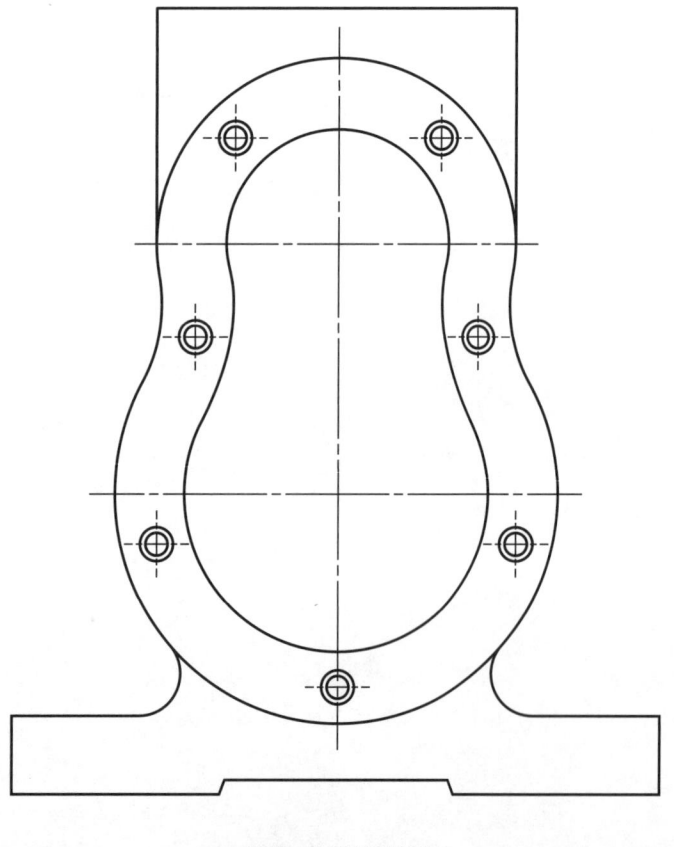

END ELEVATION

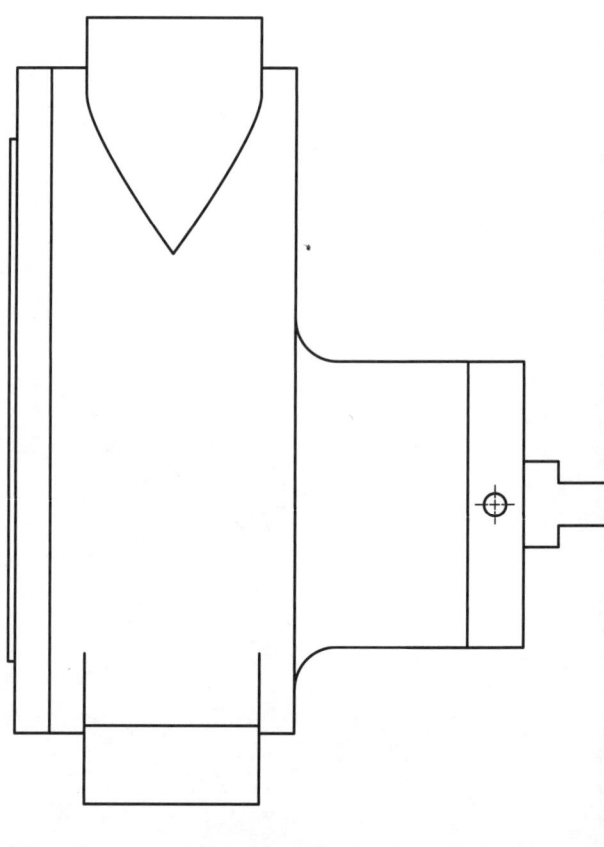

ELEVATION

SQA EXAM PAPER 2017   35   HIGHER GRAPHIC COMMUNICATION

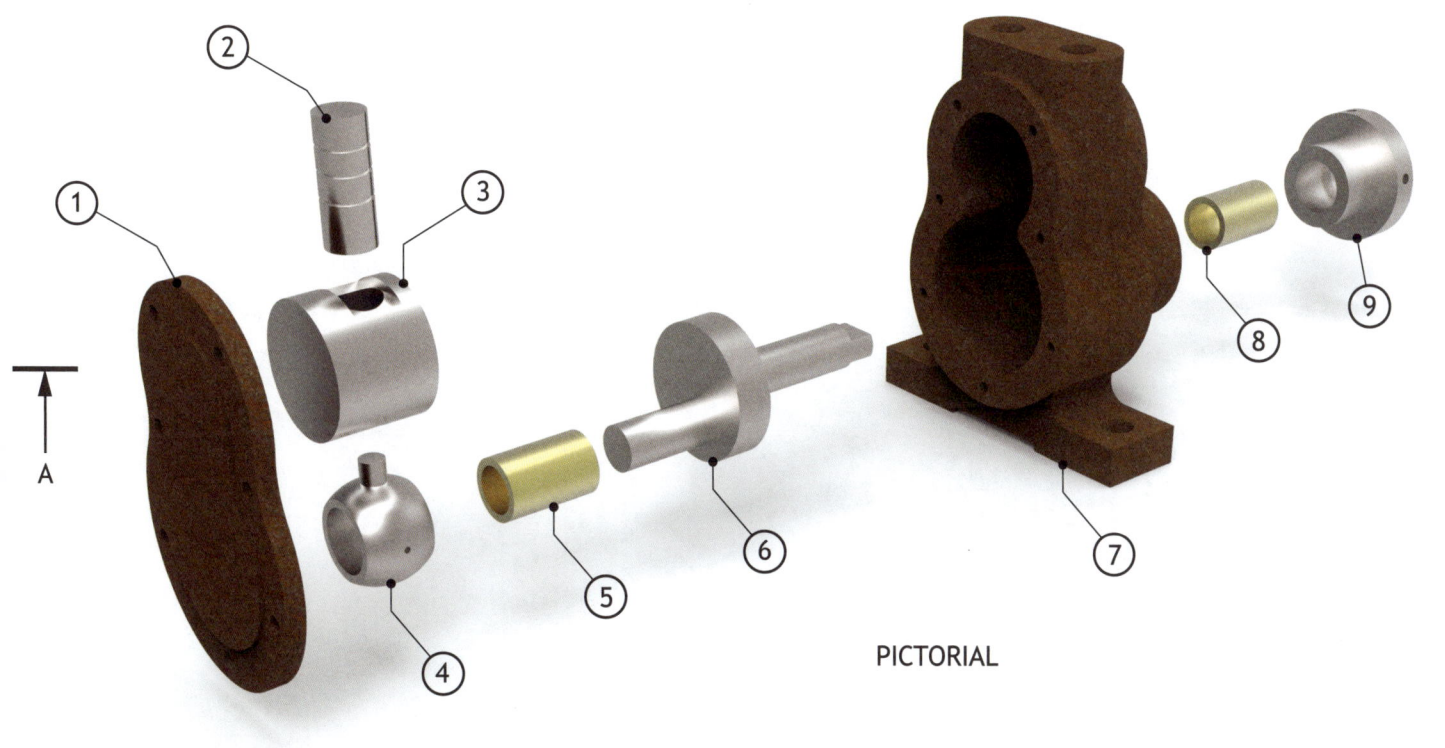

PICTORIAL

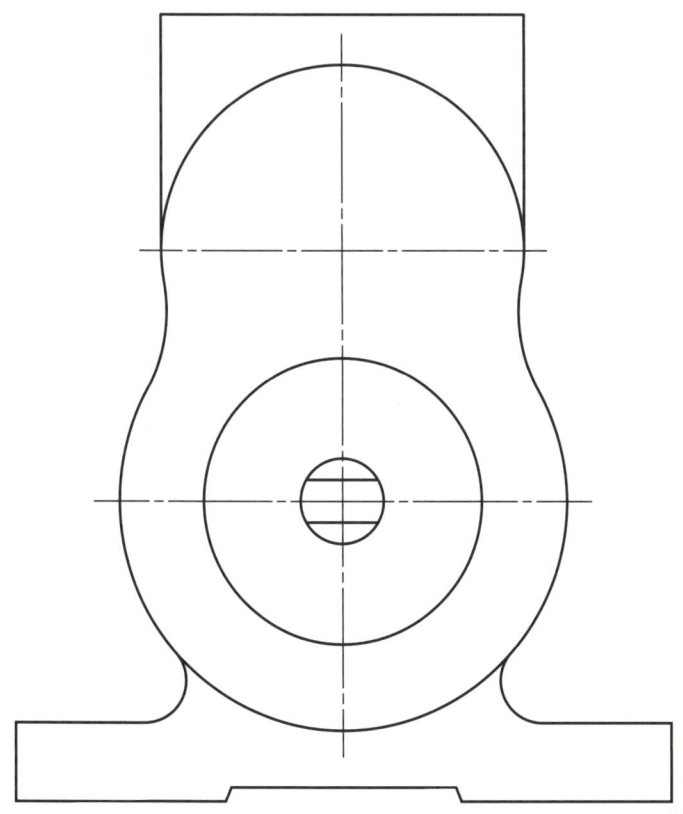

END ELEVATION

DRAWING TITLE	ASSEMBLY
QUESTION TITLE	OIL PUMP
COURSE	HIGHER GRAPHIC COMMUNICATION
DATE	
SCALE	NTS
SHEET	1/1

SQA   ALL SIZES IN MM   DO NOT SCALE

Page three

[BLANK PAGE]

DO NOT WRITE ON THIS PAGE

HIGHER

2018

FOR OFFICIAL USE

National Qualifications 2018

Mark

X735/76/01   **Graphic Communication**

THURSDAY, 10 MAY
1:00 PM – 3:00 PM

Fill in these boxes and read what is printed below.

Full name of centre

Town

Forename(s)

Surname

Number of seat

Date of birth
Day   Month   Year   Scottish candidate number

Total marks — 70

Attempt ALL questions.

All dimensions are in mm.

All technical sketches and drawings use third angle projection.

You may use rulers, compasses or trammels for measuring.

In all questions you may use sketches and annotations to support your answer if you wish.

Write your answers clearly in the spaces provided in this booklet. Additional space for answers is provided at the end of this booklet. If you use this space you must clearly identify the question number you are attempting.

Use **blue** or **black** ink.

Before leaving the examination room you must give this booklet to the Invigilator; if you do not, you may lose all the marks for this paper.

SQA

Total marks — 70

Attempt ALL questions

1. An exploded view and an assembled view of a tablet stand are shown below.

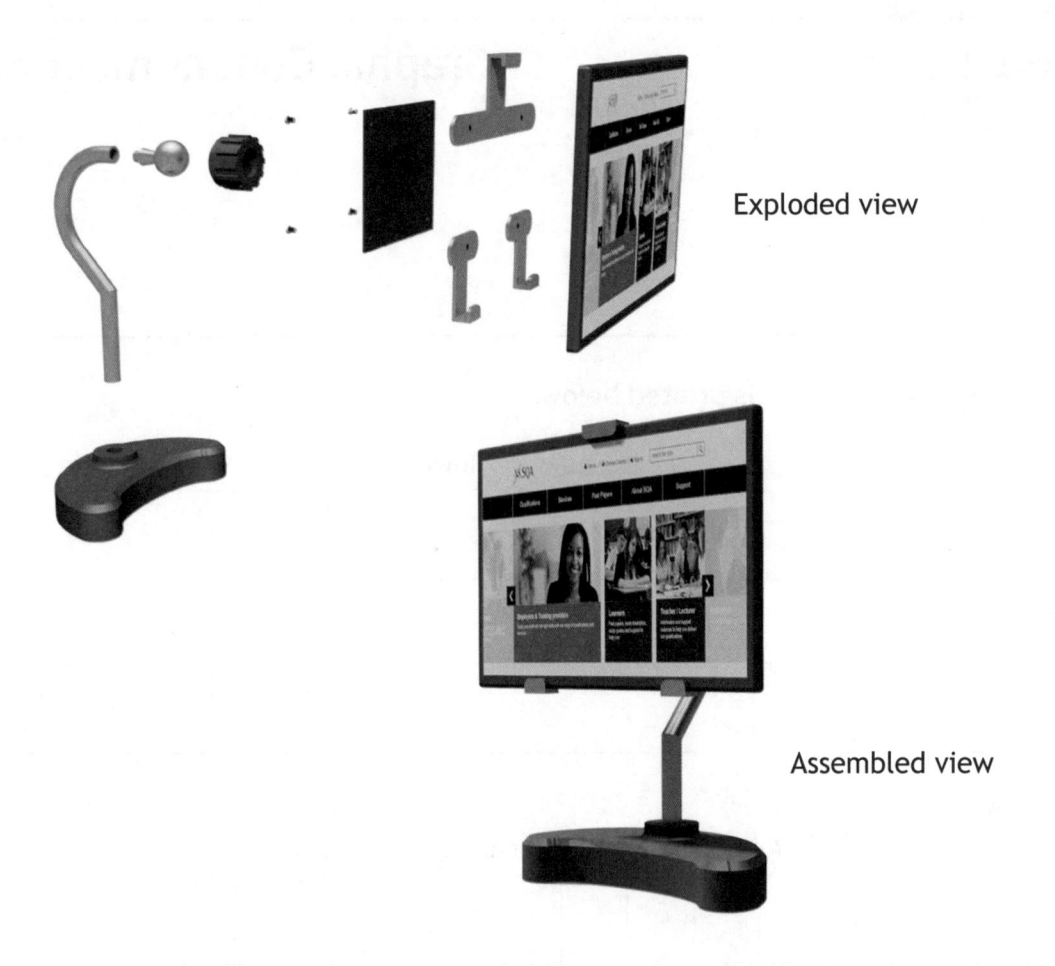

Exploded view

Assembled view

The tablet stand was designed using **bottom up modelling**.

(a) Explain the term **bottom up modelling** in relation to the assembled tablet stand.

2

1. (continued)

(b) The base for the tablet stand was created using tangency and ellipse construction, as shown below.

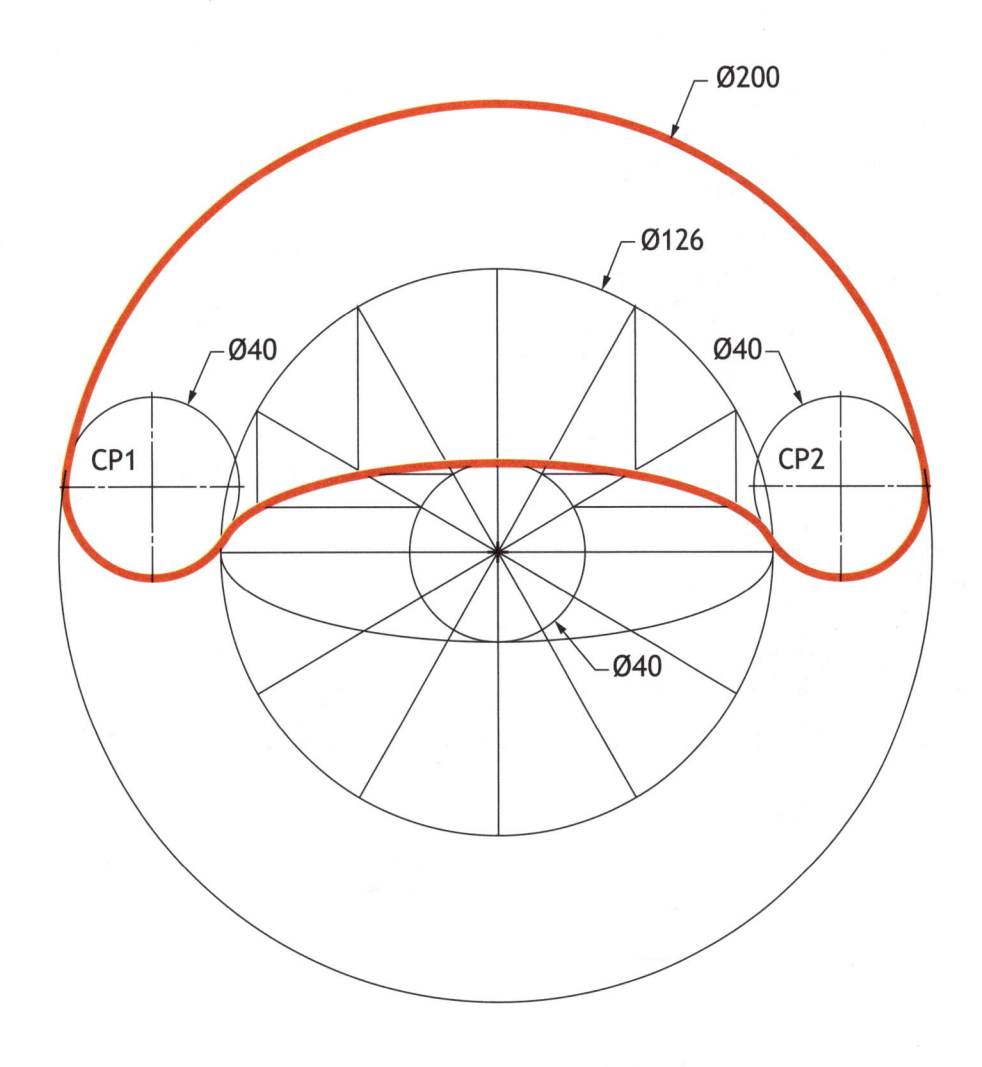

State, with reference to the 2D drawing shown above:

(i) the length of the major axis of the ellipse; **1**

_____

(ii) the length of the minor axis of the ellipse. **1**

_____

[Turn over

1. (continued)

   (c) The base for the tablet stand is to be modelled using 3D CAD. A 2D production drawing of the tablet stand is shown below.

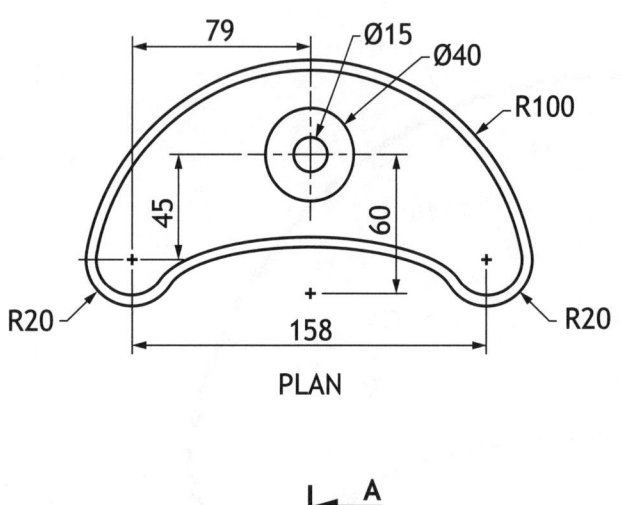

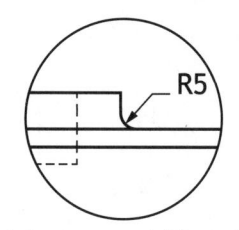

   PLAN

   Enlargement View **B**

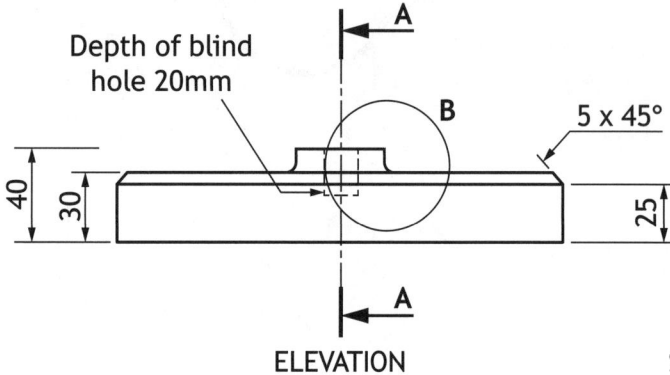

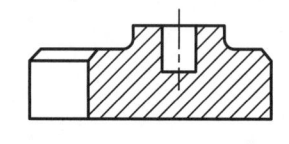

   ELEVATION

   SECTIONAL END ELEVATION ON **A-A**

1. (c) (continued)

Describe the 3D CAD modelling techniques used to create this component. You must make reference to the dimensions shown in the 2D production drawing opposite.

You may use sketches to support your answer. 4

[Turn over

1. (continued)

   (d) A pictorial view of the support arm for the tablet stand is shown below. Also shown is a 2D production drawing.

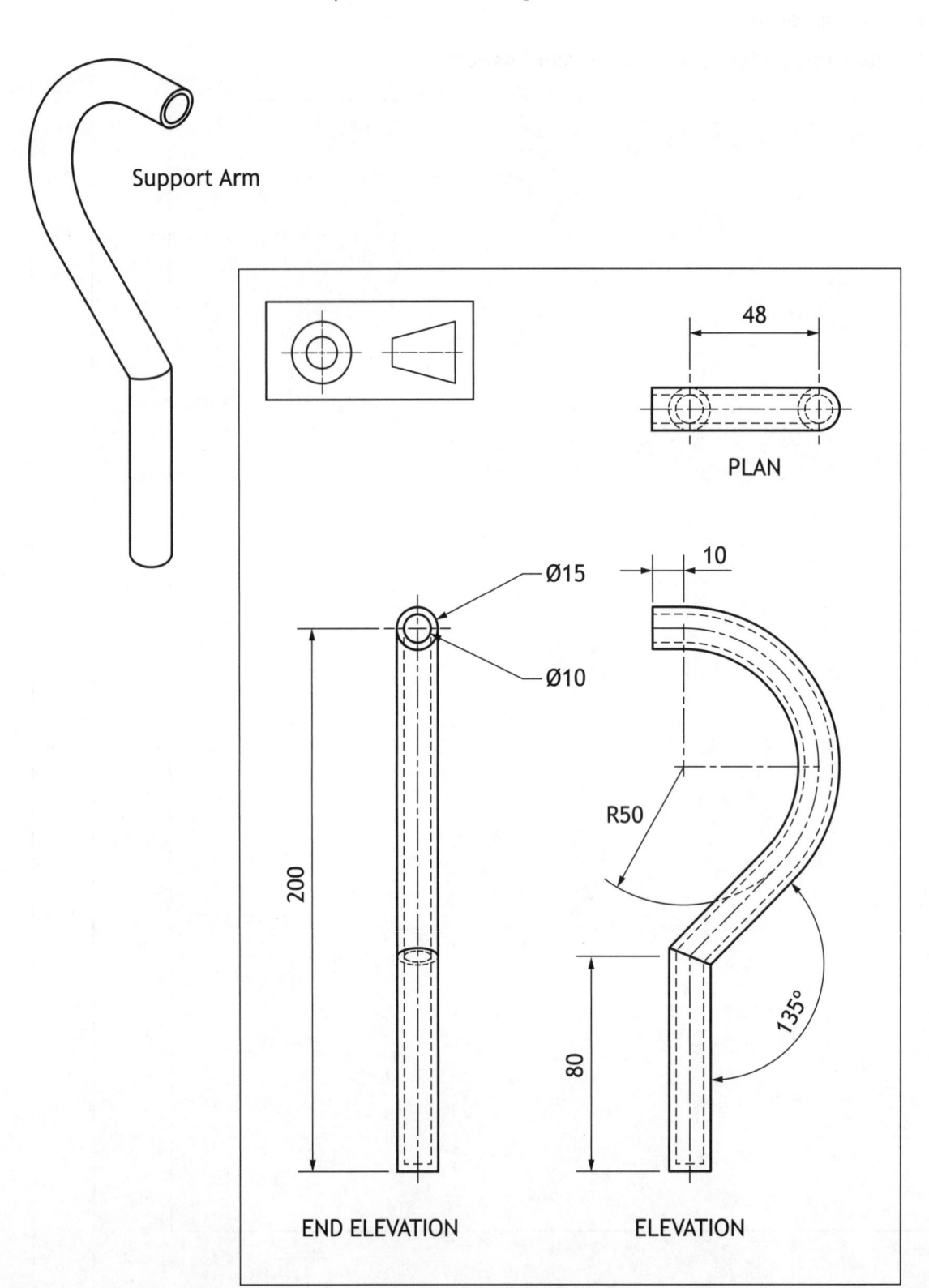

   Support Arm

   PLAN

   48

   Ø15
   Ø10
   10
   R50
   200
   80
   135°

   END ELEVATION   ELEVATION

1. (d) (continued)

Describe the 3D CAD modelling techniques used to create the support arm. You must make reference to the dimensions shown in the 2D production drawing opposite.

You may use sketches to support your answer.

3

[Turn over

1. (continued)

   (e) A pictorial view of the ball joint for the tablet stand is shown below. Also shown is a 2D production drawing.

   Describe the **single** 3D CAD modelling technique used to create the ball joint component. You must refer to the dimensions given in the drawing shown below.

   You may use sketches to illustrate your answer.

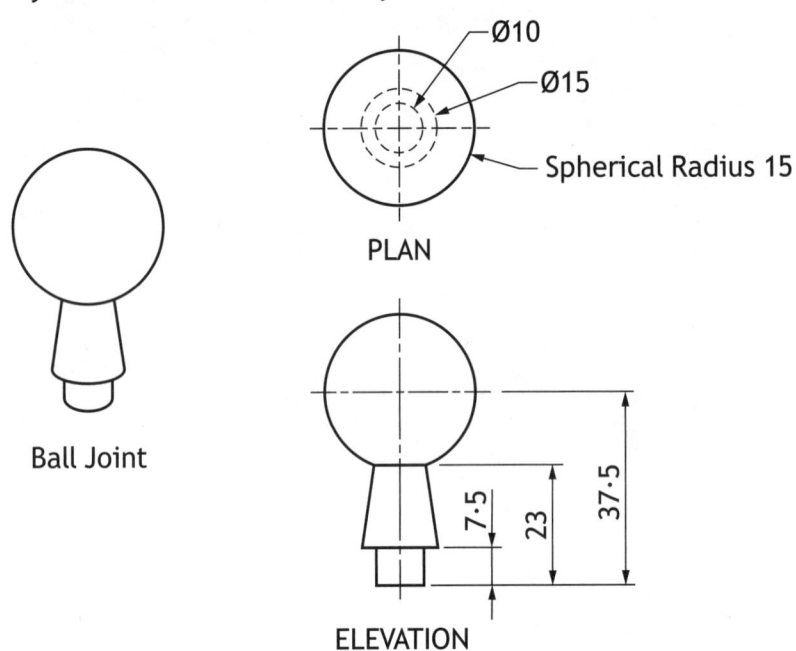

   3

   PLAN
   - Ø10
   - Ø15
   - Spherical Radius 15

   Ball Joint

   ELEVATION
   - 7·5
   - 23
   - 37·5

   In order for the ball joint to work effectively a functional tolerance needs to be applied to it.

   (f) Using British Standard conventions, apply a diameter tolerance of 10 mm +0·15 and −0·25 to the graphic below.

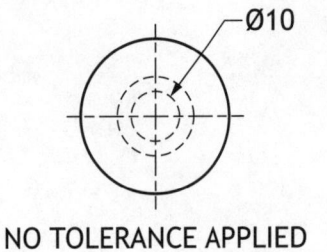

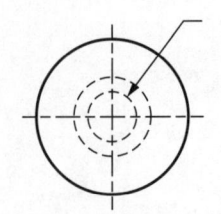

   2

   NO TOLERANCE APPLIED — Ø10

   TOLERANCE APPLIED

1. (continued)

   (g) Two pictorial views of the ball socket for the tablet stand are shown below. Grips were added to help the user adjust the angle of the tablet. Also shown is a 2D production drawing.

   Describe the 3D CAD techniques used to create the **grips** on the ball socket component. You must refer to the dimensions given in the drawings shown below.

   You may use sketches to support your answer.

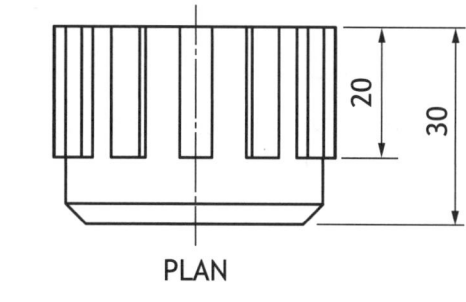

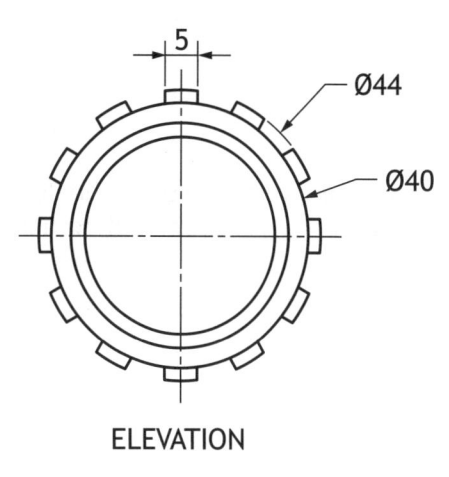

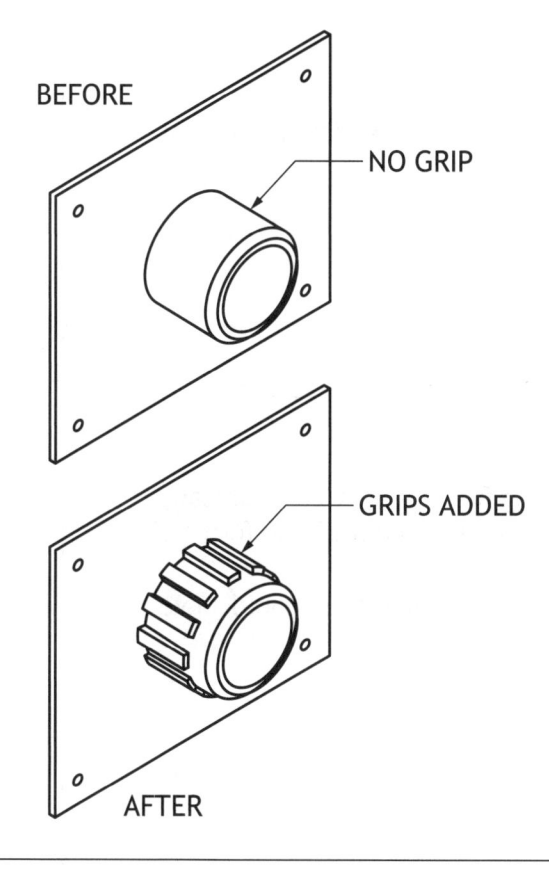

   3

   BEFORE — NO GRIP

   GRIPS ADDED

   AFTER

   PLAN

   ELEVATION

   Ø44
   Ø40
   5
   20
   30

1. (continued)

   (h) When reviewing the final model of the ball socket, the CAD technician decided to reduce the number of grips on the ball socket from 12 to 10.

   (i) Describe how the modelling tree is used to edit the number of grips. **1**

   (ii) Explain why editing the modelling tree is an efficient way of changing the number of grips. **1**

2. A product is manufactured abroad. The 3D modelling files are sent electronically to the manufacturer. The 3D modelling files will be sent in the IGES file format.

   (a) (i) Name another suitable 3D modelling file format that could have been used. **1**

   (ii) Explain why using these file formats is advantageous to the manufacturer. **1**

2. (continued)

The manufacturer has also requested that the production drawings are sent electronically.

(b) Explain why it is advantageous to the manufacturer to receive a vector graphic rather than a raster graphic. **1**

(c) The production drawings are created by CAD technicians and include several components from a CAD library.

Describe two benefits a CAD library offers a CAD technician. **2**

(d) (i) State the name of the British Standard symbol shown below. **1**

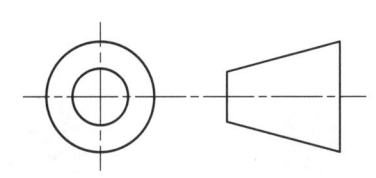

(ii) Explain why this symbol is useful to the manufacturer. **1**

[Turn over

3. Two different types of graphics are shown below.

Promotional

Production

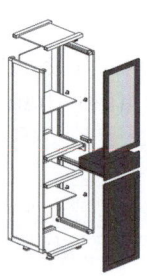

(a) Explain the purpose of each of the graphics shown.

   (i) Promotional

_____

_____

_____

   (ii) Production

_____

_____

_____

(b) A customer used a popular kitchen design website to quickly generate a range of initial designs for the layout of their kitchen, as shown above.

Describe two advantages of using digital methods compared to manual sketching methods at this stage in the process.

_____

_____

_____

_____

_____

Page twelve

4. Graphics for a spotlight are shown below.

The spotlight casing (part 6) has two raised bosses to allow the mounting bracket (part 4) to be screwed on.

You must refer to the supplementary sheet for use with question 4, provided, to answer all parts of this question.

(a) Calculate the size for dimension X for the boss shown below.

Maximum size of X _____ mm

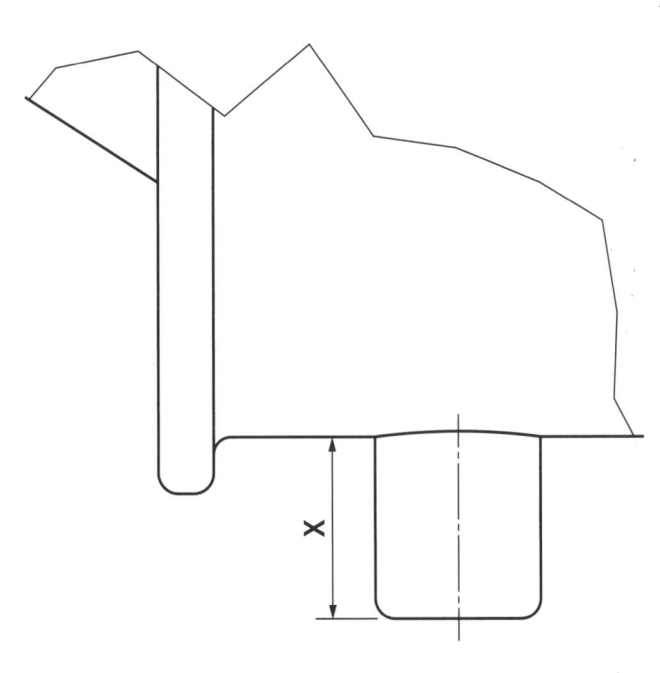

ENLARGED PARTIAL VIEW A

[Turn over

4. (continued)

(b) An elevation and end elevation of the spotlight are given below.

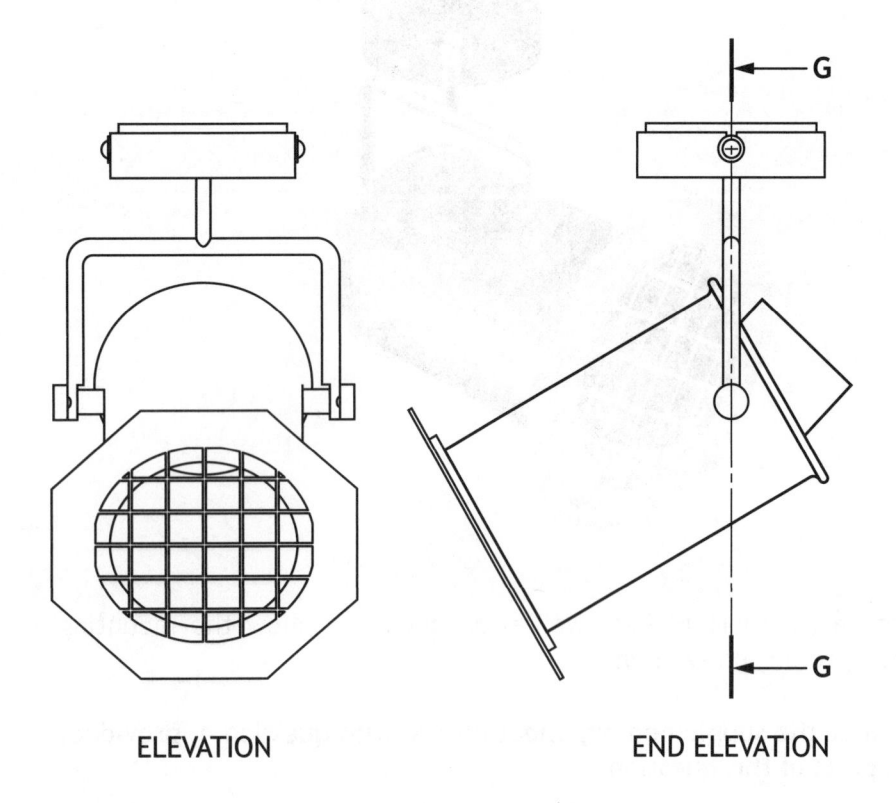

ELEVATION   END ELEVATION

(i) A partial view of section G–G is shown below.

Apply hatching to this drawing in accordance with British Standard conventions.

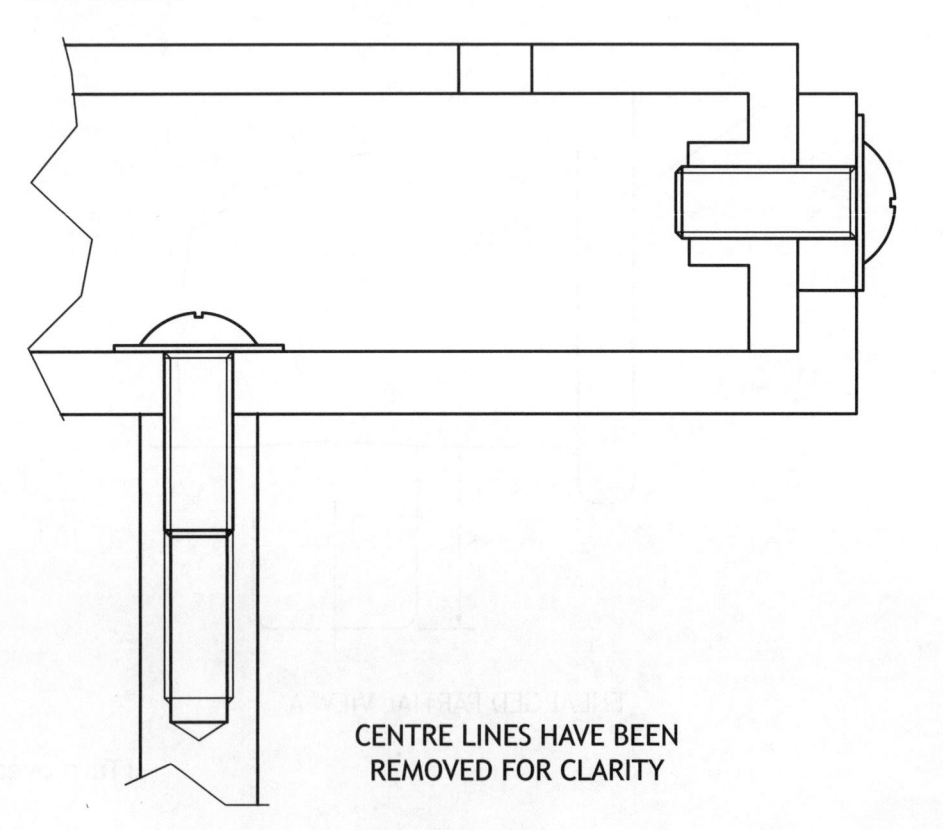

4

CENTRE LINES HAVE BEEN REMOVED FOR CLARITY

4. (b) (continued)

(ii) The thumb screws are available with two types of grips on the heads, **straight knurling** or **diamond knurling**.

Apply the British Standard convention for each type of knurling below.

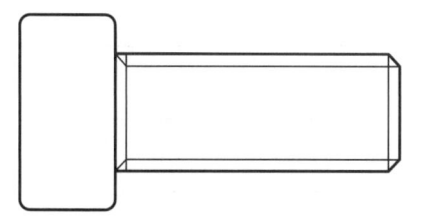

STRAIGHT KNURLING 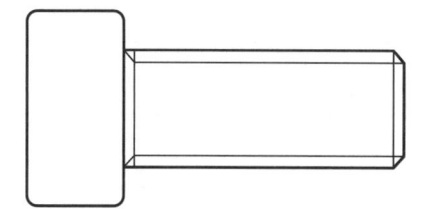   DIAMOND KNURLING

(c) The thumb screws are replaced with hand screws, which are easier for the user to grip. A rendered illustration and front elevation for the hand screw are shown below.

RENDERED ILLUSTRATION OF HAND SCREW

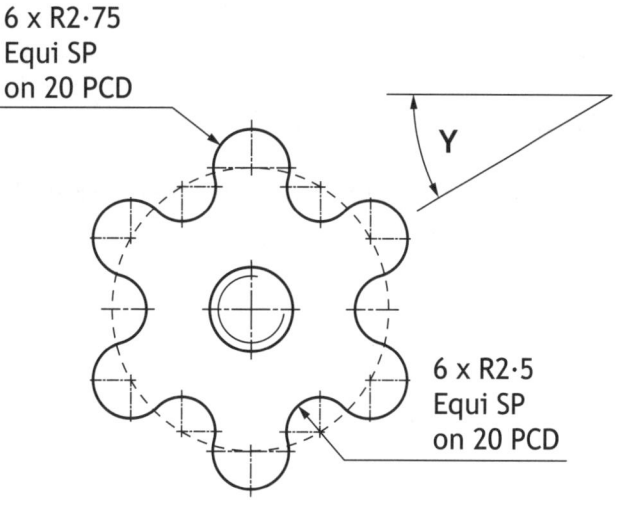

6 x R2·75 Equi SP on 20 PCD

6 x R2·5 Equi SP on 20 PCD

ELEVATION

(i) State what PCD stands for in the drawing above.

(ii) Calculate the angle Y shown in the drawing above.

[Turn over

Page fifteen

5. Use the draft infographic on the **supplementary sheet for use with question 5**, provided, to answer all parts of this question.

   A graphic artist has produced a draft infographic, which gives readers advice on how to save money on their energy bills.

   (a) Describe how the graphic artist has used **shape** to create **rhythm**. 2

   (b) Explain why the graphic artist's use of **grid structure** is of benefit to the reader. 2

   (c) Describe how the graphic artist has created **unity** throughout the graphic. 2

   (d) Describe how the graphic artist has created **depth** in the graphic. 2

MARKS DO NOT WRITE IN THIS MARGIN

5. (continued)

(e) Describe how the graphic artist has used **alignment** in the graphic. 2

(f) Describe how the graphic artist has created **emphasis** in the graphic. 2

[Turn over

6. A company already has a large client base for its printed publications and wants to expand to an online style magazine.

   (a) State two advantages to the consumer, other than cost, of an online publication when compared with a printed publication. **2**

   (b) The company will launch an online magazine with the option to view in a variety of languages.

   Describe how this feature would be of benefit to the company. **1**

   (c) The online magazine will be available across a variety of electronic devices.

   Explain why the choice of **typeface** is an important aspect for the company to consider when creating the online magazine. **2**

6. (continued)

(d) When choosing the typeface, the graphic designers considered different **serif** and **sans serif** fonts.

Describe the main characteristics of **serif** fonts. **1**

You may use sketches to support your answer.

(e) The company stores its graphics library in the cloud.

Describe **two** advantages of cloud based storage for graphic designers. **2**

[Turn over

6. **(continued)**

Use the desktop published magazine page on the **supplementary sheet for use with question 6 (f)–(j)**, provided, to answer the following questions.

(f) Explain how the following DTP features have been used on the desktop published magazine page.

    (i) Transparency   **1**

    (ii) Colour picking   **1**

(g) A **drop cap** has been used on the desktop published magazine page.

Explain the purpose of a **drop cap**.   **2**

(h) **Reverse** has been used on the desktop published magazine page.

Describe the use of **reverse** in the desktop published magazine page.   **2**

6. (continued)

(i) The graphic designer has used different types of **justification** on the desktop published magazine page.

Explain why the designer has chosen to do this for the main body text. **1**

(j) **Line** has been used on the desktop published magazine page.

Describe how the use of **line** has been used to enhance the desktop published magazine page. **2**

[END OF QUESTION PAPER]

ADDITIONAL SPACE FOR ANSWERS

ADDITIONAL SPACE FOR ANSWERS

H National Qualifications 2018

X735/76/11

Graphic Communication Supplementary Sheets

THURSDAY, 10 MAY
1:00 PM — 3:00 PM

Supplementary sheets for use with questions 4 (a), 5 and 6 (f)–(j).

Supplementary sheet for use with question 4 (a)

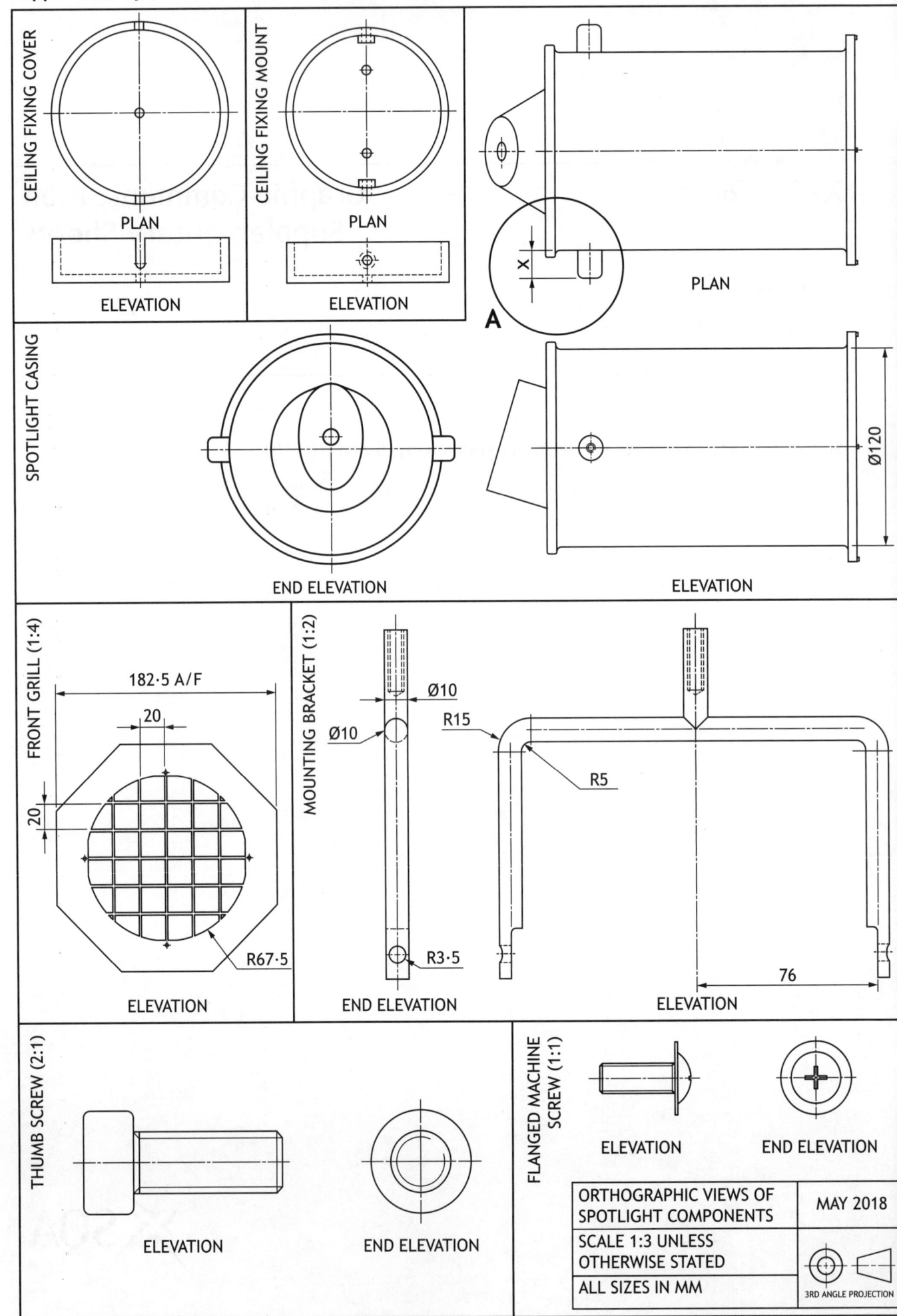

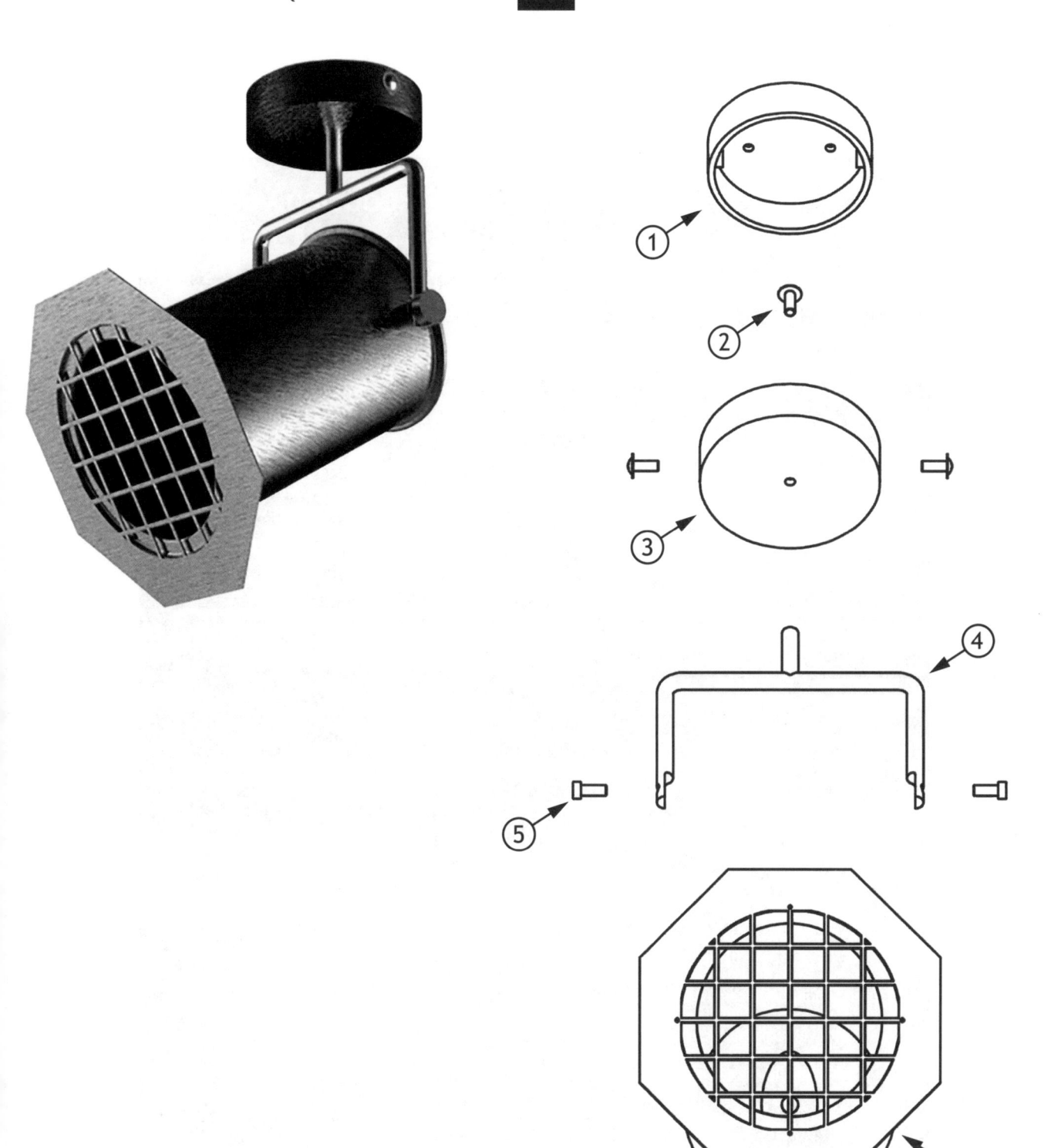

PARTS LIST		
PART NO.	PART NAME	NO. OF PARTS
1	CEILING FIXING MOUNT	1
2	FLANGED MACHINE SCREW	3
3	FIXING COVER	1
4	MOUNTING BRACKET	1
5	THUMB SCREW	2
6	SPOTLIGHT CASING AND GRILL	1

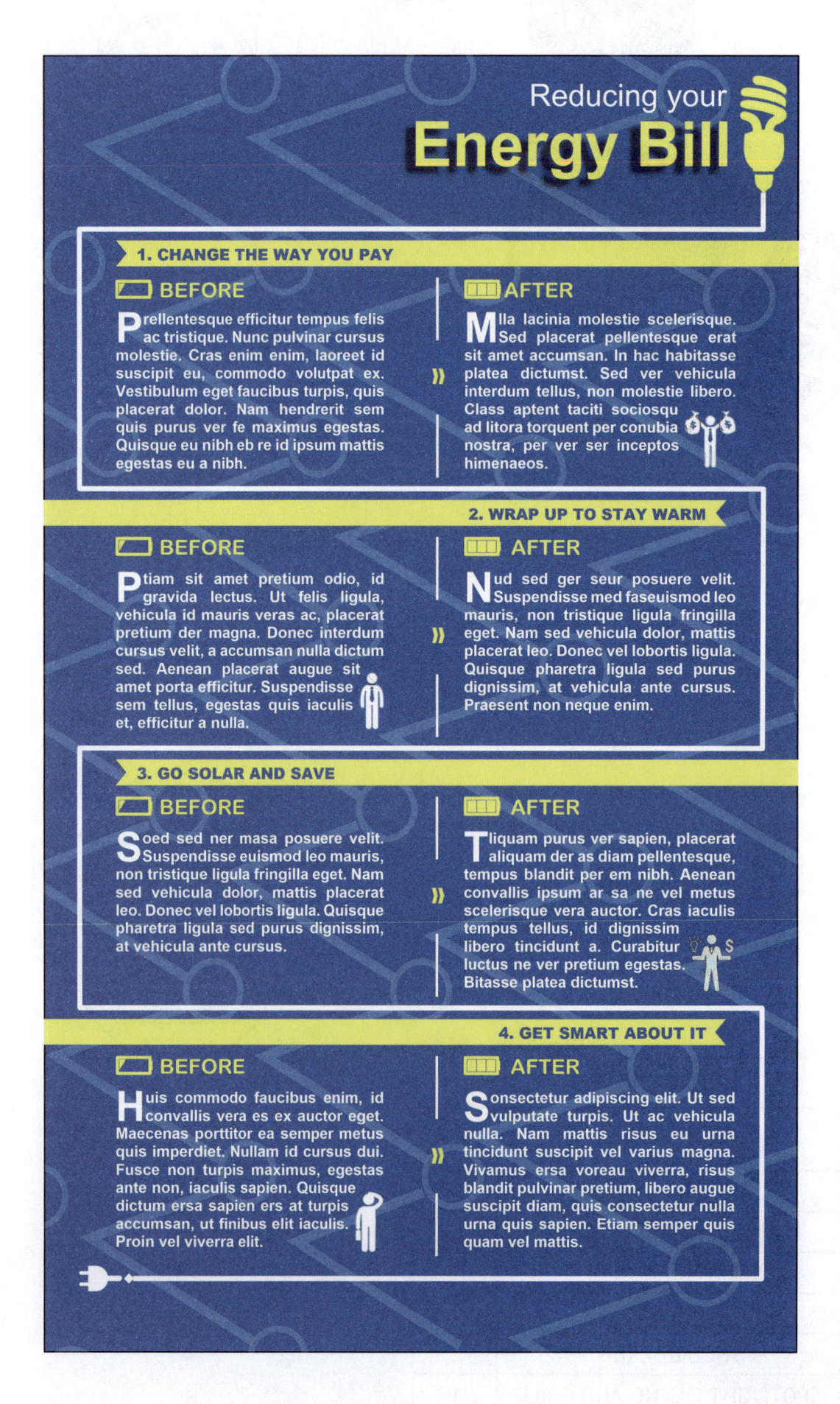

Supplementary sheet for use with question 5

Infographic

Reducing your Energy Bill

1. CHANGE THE WAY YOU PAY

BEFORE

Pellentesque efficitur tempus felis ac tristique. Nunc pulvinar cursus molestie. Cras enim enim, laoreet id suscipit eu, commodo volutpat ex. Vestibulum eget faucibus turpis, quis placerat dolor. Nam hendrerit sem quis purus ver fe maximus egestas. Quisque eu nibh eb re id ipsum mattis egestas eu a nibh.

AFTER

Mlla lacinia molestie scelerisque. Sed placerat pellentesque erat sit amet accumsan. In hac habitasse platea dictumst. Sed ver vehicula interdum tellus, non molestie libero. Class aptent taciti sociosqu ad litora torquent per conubia nostra, per ver ser inceptos himenaeos.

2. WRAP UP TO STAY WARM

BEFORE

Ptiam sit amet pretium odio, id gravida lectus. Ut felis ligula, vehicula id mauris veras ac, placerat pretium der magna. Donec interdum cursus velit, a accumsan nulla dictum sed. Aenean placerat augue sit amet porta efficitur. Suspendisse sem tellus, egestas quis iaculis et, efficitur a nulla.

AFTER

Nud sed ger seur posuere velit. Suspendisse med faseuismod leo mauris, non tristique ligula fringilla eget. Nam sed vehicula dolor, mattis placerat leo. Donec vel lobortis ligula. Quisque pharetra ligula sed purus dignissim, at vehicula ante cursus. Praesent non neque enim.

3. GO SOLAR AND SAVE

BEFORE

Soed sed ner masa posuere velit. Suspendisse euismod leo mauris, non tristique ligula fringilla eget. Nam sed vehicula dolor, mattis placerat leo. Donec vel lobortis ligula. Quisque pharetra ligula sed purus dignissim, at vehicula ante cursus.

AFTER

Tliquam purus ver sapien, placerat aliquam der as diam pellentesque, tempus blandit per em nibh. Aenean convallis ipsum ar sa ne vel metus scelerisque vera auctor. Cras iaculis tempus tellus, id dignissim libero tincidunt a. Curabitur luctus ne ver pretium egestas. Bitasse platea dictumst.

4. GET SMART ABOUT IT

BEFORE

Huis commodo faucibus enim, id convallis vera es ex auctor eget. Maecenas porttitor ea semper metus quis imperdiet. Nullam id cursus dui. Fusce non turpis maximus, egestas ante non, iaculis sapien. Quisque dictum ersa sapien ers at turpis accumsan, ut finibus elit iaculis. Proin vel viverra elit.

AFTER

Sonsectetur adipiscing elit. Ut sed vulputate turpis. Ut ac vehicula nulla. Nam mattis risus eu urna tincidunt suscipit vel varius magna. Vivamus ersa voreau vivera, risus blandit pulvinar pretium, libero augue suscipit diam, quis consectetur nulla urna quis sapien. Etiam semper quis quam vel mattis.

Page four

Supplementary sheet for use with question 6 (f)–(j)

Desktop published magazine page

Produit:Paris | Editor's word

Bright Spark!

Nulla vestibulum eleifend nulla. Suspendisse potenti. Aliquam turpis nisi, venenatis non, accumsan nec, imperdiet laoreet, lacus. In purus est, mattis eget, imperdiet nec, fermentum congue, tortor. Aenean ut nibh. Nullam hendrerit viverra dolor. Vestibulum fringilla, lectus id viverra malesuada, enim mi adipiscing ligula, et bibendum lacus lectus id sem. Cras risus turpis, varius ac, feugiat id, faucibus vitae, massa. Nunc gravida nonummy felis. Etiam suscipit, est sit amet suscipit sodales, est neque suscipit erat, nec suscipit sem enim eget leo. In porttitor rutrum leo. Ut eget leo.

Nulla quis nibh. Proin ac pede vel ligula facilisis gravida. Phasellus purus. Etiam sapien. Duis diam urna, iaculis ut, vehicula ac, varius sit amet, mi. Donec id nisl. Aliquam erat volutpat. Integer fringilla. Duis lobortis, quam non volutpat suscipit, magna sem consequat libero, ac hendrerit urna ante id mi. Quisque commodo facilisis tellus. Integer sodales lorem sed nisl. Morbi consectetuer mauris quis odio. Ut dolor lorem, viverra vitae, viverra eu, euismod nec, enim. Lorem ipsum dolor sit amet, consectetuer adipiscing elit.

Morbi nisl eros, dignissim nec, malesuada et, convallis quis, augue. Vestibulum ante ipsum primis in faucibus orci luctus et ultrices posuere cubilia Curae; Proin aliquam, leo at luctus tempus, eros lectus eleifend massa, quis sollicitudin erat magna non leo. Vestibulum vel metus. Donec sagittis velit vel augue. Fusce in nisl vitae massa venenatis rhoncus. Praesent orci velit, lobortis eget, suscipit semper, congue eu, est. Quisque malesuada volutpat enim. Vestibulum leo sem, molestie a, mattis bibendum, feugiat facilisis, nisl. Nam scelerisque odio. Suspendisse fermentum faucibus felis. Praesent pharetra. In consequat felis in tellus. In mi enim, rhoncus ullamcorper, sagittis at, placerat eget, mauris.

C. Findlay

Best wishes
Calum Findlay
Editor

Produit Paris

Inside this month's issue:

congue ac, faucibus ut, erat. Donec sit amet neque. Donec posuere tempus massa. Duis vulputate mauris sit amet purus. Duis vestibulum.

Vestibulum semper enim non eros. Sed vitae arcu. Aliquam erat volutpat. nisl, suscipit at, rhoncus sit amet, porttitor sit , leo. Aenean hendrerit est. Etiam ac augue. Morbi tincidunt neque.

Morbi nisl eros, dignissim nec, malesuada et, convallis quis, augue. Vestibulum ipsum primis in faucibus luctus et ultrices posuere cubilia Curae; Proin aliquam, leo at.

Produit:Parisonline.com

1 | Produit:Paris | issue 120

[BLANK PAGE]

HIGHER

2018 Specimen Question Paper

FOR OFFICIAL USE

H

**National Qualifications
SPECIMEN ONLY**

Mark

S835/76/01 **Graphic Communication**

Date — Not applicable
Duration — 2 hour 30 minutes

Fill in these boxes and read what is printed below.

Full name of centre

Town

Forename(s)

Surname

Number of seat

Date of birth
Day   Month   Year

Scottish candidate number

Total marks — 90

Attempt ALL questions.

All dimensions are in mm.

All technical sketches and drawings use third angle projection.

You may use rulers, compasses or trammels for measuring.

In all questions you may use sketches and annotations to support your answer if you wish.

Write your answers clearly in the spaces provided in this booklet. Additional space for answers is provided at the end of this booklet. If you use this space you must clearly identify the question number you are attempting.

Use **blue** or **black** ink.

Before leaving the examination room you must give this booklet to the Invigilator; if you do not, you may lose all the marks for this paper.

SQA

Total marks — 90

Attempt ALL questions

1. A CAD technician created the 3D CAD model of an electric guitar.

   The technician made use of a **CAD library** in the production of the guitar 3D CAD model.

   (a) Describe **two** benefits of using a CAD library.   2

   _____

   _____

   _____

   _____

   _____

   _____

   (b) The 3D CAD model of the guitar will be used to create production and promotional graphics.

   Describe **one** benefit of using 3D CAD models in:

   (i) advertising   1

   _____

   _____

   (ii) manufacturing   1

   _____

   _____

1. (continued)

An exploded view and a partial enlargement of the guitar are shown below.

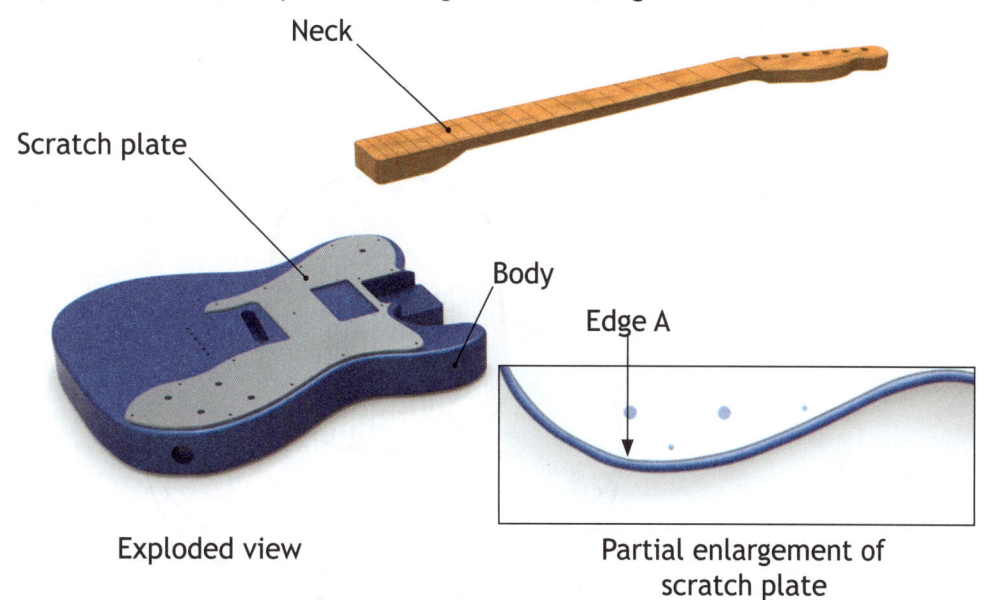

Exploded view

Partial enlargement of scratch plate

(c) The CAD technician used the process of **top down modelling** to ensure the neck would fit with the body.

Describe the process of **top down modelling**. **2**

You may use sketches to support your answer.

(d) The CAD technician wanted the scratch plate to follow the same shape as the body.

(i) State the name of the 2D CAD tool used to ensure the scratch plate was the same shape as the guitar body at **Edge A**, shown above. **1**

(ii) Describe how this 2D CAD tool was used. **1**

You may use sketches to support your answer.

1. (continued)

A production drawing for a control dial for the guitar is shown below.

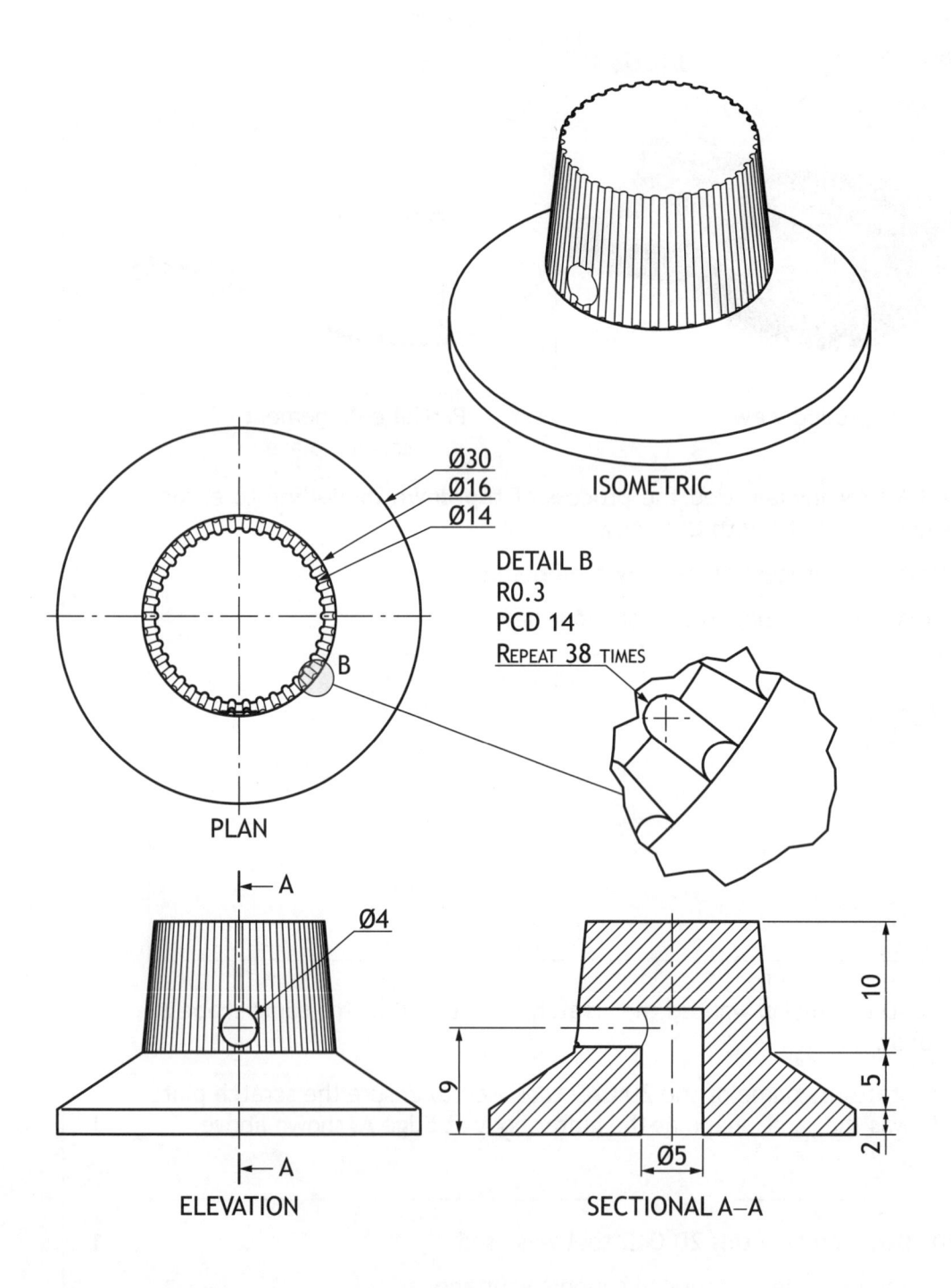

ISOMETRIC

Ø30
Ø16
Ø14

DETAIL B
R0.3
PCD 14
REPEAT 38 TIMES

PLAN

Ø4

ELEVATION

Ø5
10
9
5
2

SECTIONAL A–A

1. (continued)

   (e) Describe the 3D CAD modelling techniques required to produce the control dial. You must refer to the dimensions given in the production drawing.

   8

   You may use sketches to support your answer.

1. (continued)

   An incomplete elevation and a rendered pictorial drawing of a component of the guitar are shown below.

   (f) Sketch the British Standard conventions in the correct location on the incomplete elevation for:

   (i) thread **1**

   (ii) flat on shaft **1**

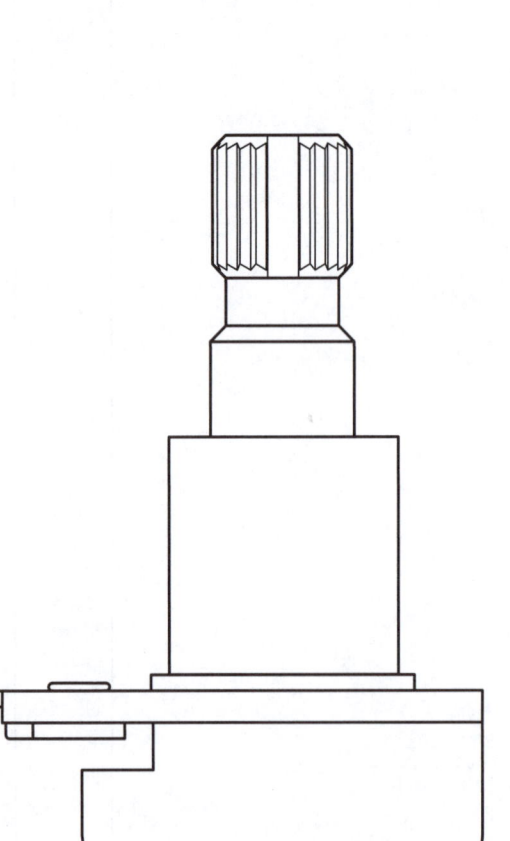

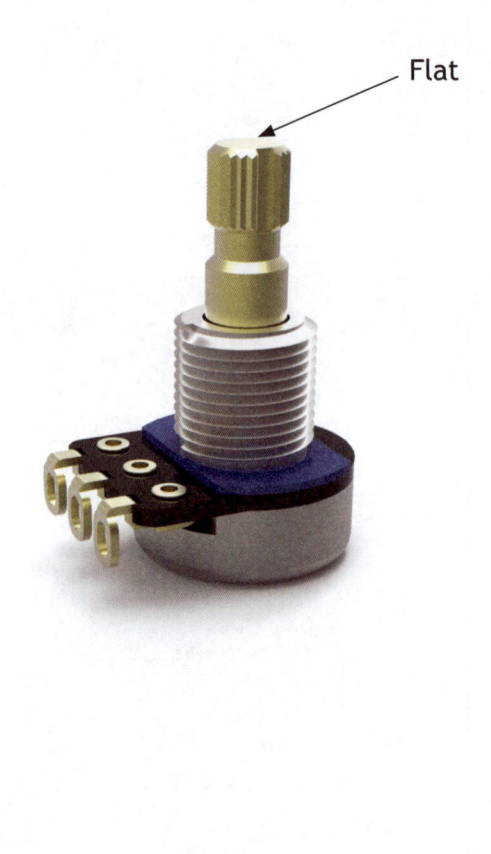

   Flat

1. **(continued)**

   (g) Look at the guitar headstock shown below. The CAD technician modelled the headstock using the principles of tangency.

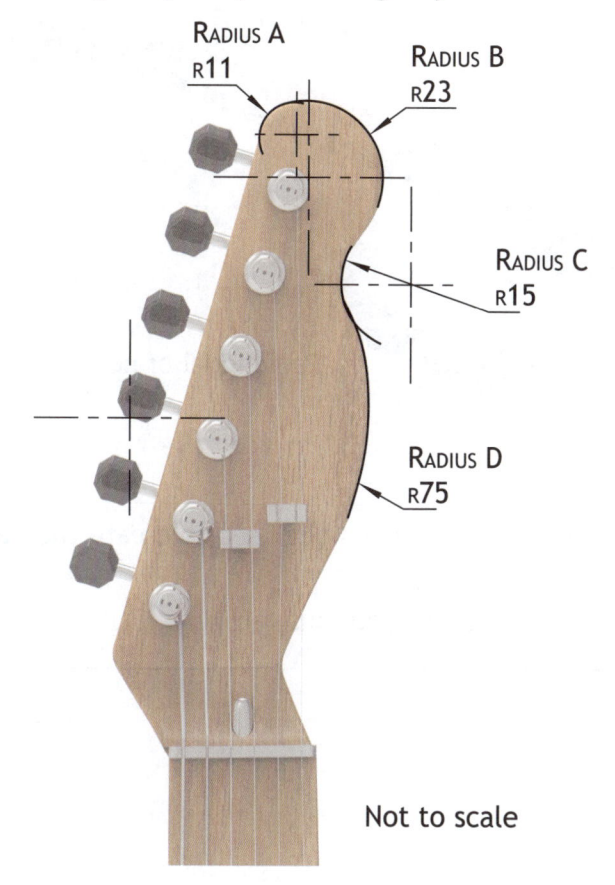

   RADIUS A R11
   RADIUS B R23
   RADIUS C R15
   RADIUS D R75

   Not to scale

   (i) Calculate the distance from the centre of **radius C** to the centre of **radius D**.

   (ii) Calculate the distance from the centre of **radius A** to the centre of **radius B**.

1. (continued)

   (h) The 3D CAD model of the guitar neck and a part model are shown below.

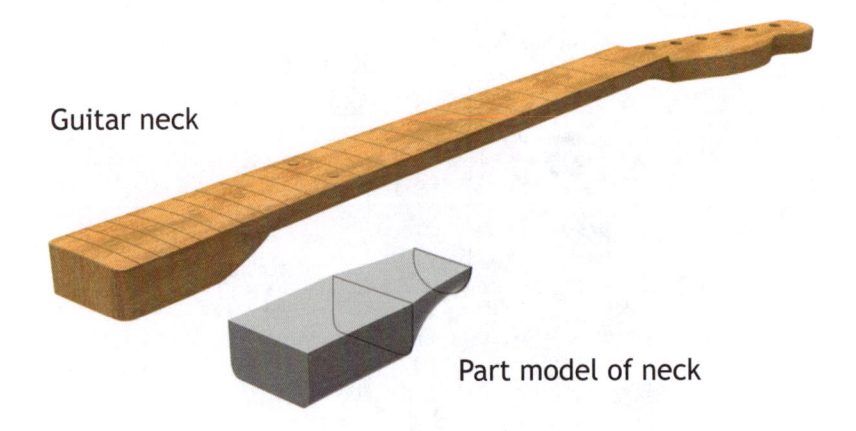

   Guitar neck

   Part model of neck

   Describe the 3D CAD modelling technique used to create the part model of the neck.

   You may use sketches to support your answer.

   3

2. A fashion magazine is producing an article on sunglasses. A graphic designer created a draft layout for the article shown below.

(a) Describe the effects the graphic designer has created in the layout by using the following.

   (i) White space

   (ii) Colour

2. (a) (continued)

   (iii) Typeface 2

   (b) Explain how the graphic designer has used **proportion** in the layout. 4

   (c) Describe how the graphic designer has created **depth** in the layout. 2

   (d) Describe how the graphic designer has used **line** to enhance the layout. 2

2. (continued)

(e) The Ray-Ban logo is a vector file.

Explain **two** advantages of using a vector file format in the production of the layout.

2

_____

_____

_____

_____

[Turn over

2. **(continued)**

The final layout for the article is shown below.

The final layout was produced in layers using DTP software.

2. (continued)

(f) Describe **three** advantages to the graphic designer of using layers for this layout. **3**

(g) The graphic designer has used different types of justification for the sub-heading and main body text of the layout.

Explain why the graphic designer has chosen to do this for:

(i) the sub-heading **1**

(ii) the main body text **1**

[Turn over

2. (continued)

(h) The pre-press layout shown above contains crop and registration marks.

(i) Explain why the yellow boxes bleed beyond the crop marks. 1

_____

_____

(ii) Describe the purpose of registration marks in printing. 2

_____

_____

_____

_____

3. Dundee Waterfront is undergoing a £1 billion redevelopment.

The official website includes various types of graphics aimed at promoting the development to the local community. These include:

- **location plans** of the entire development
- **site plans** of some of the proposed new buildings

(a) Describe the features of **both** types of plans for providing information about the redevelopment to the local community. **4**

A selection of rendered CAD pictorial images of the new train station were uploaded to the website.

[Turn over

3. (continued)

(b) Explain **three** advantages of using rendered CAD pictorials to communicate the design to the local community. **3**

(c) The architect shared initial sketches of a building idea on the website. These sketches were created using pencil and marker pen.

  (i) Describe how the manual sketches can be converted to digital images for use on the website. **1**

  (ii) State two reasons why a **jpeg** would be a suitable file format for these images. **2**

(d) The architect also created initial digital sketches on a touch-screen tablet.

  Describe **two** advantages to the architect of using digital sketching. **2**

4. Look at the exploded CAD illustration of a castor wheel assembly shown below.

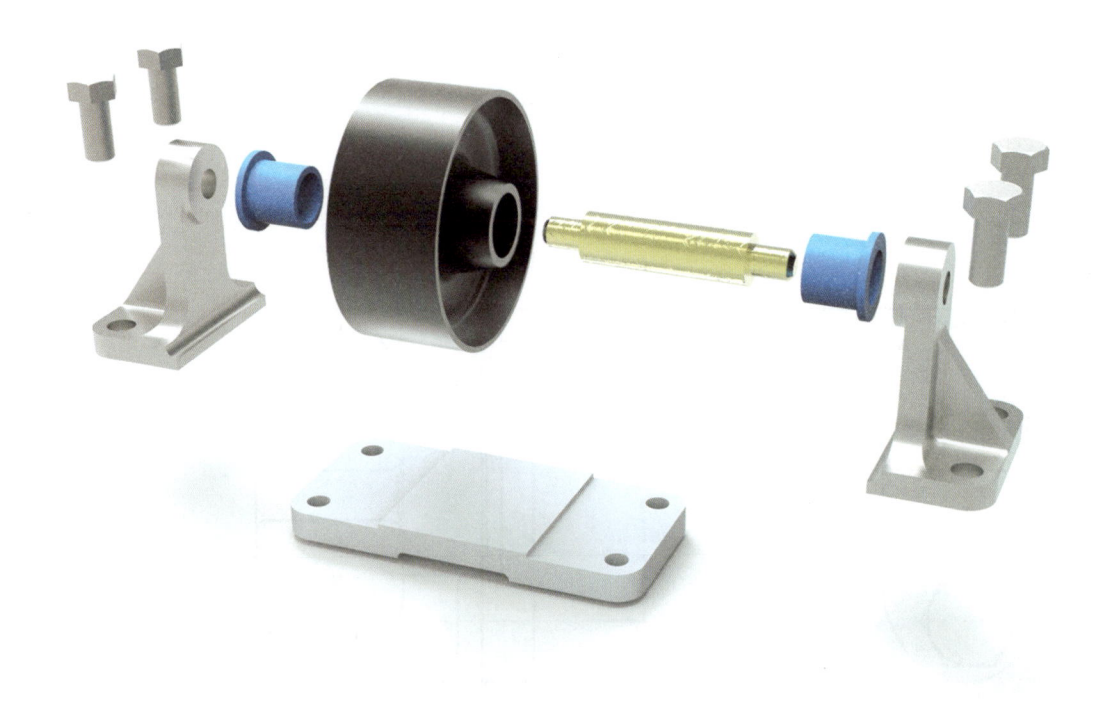

The assembly is made up of several parts that include four M12 bolts.

The **plan** and **incomplete stepped sectional elevation A-A** are shown on *Page eighteen*.

Complete section A-A by applying hatching lines to appropriate areas in accordance with British Standards.

5

[Turn over

4. (continued)

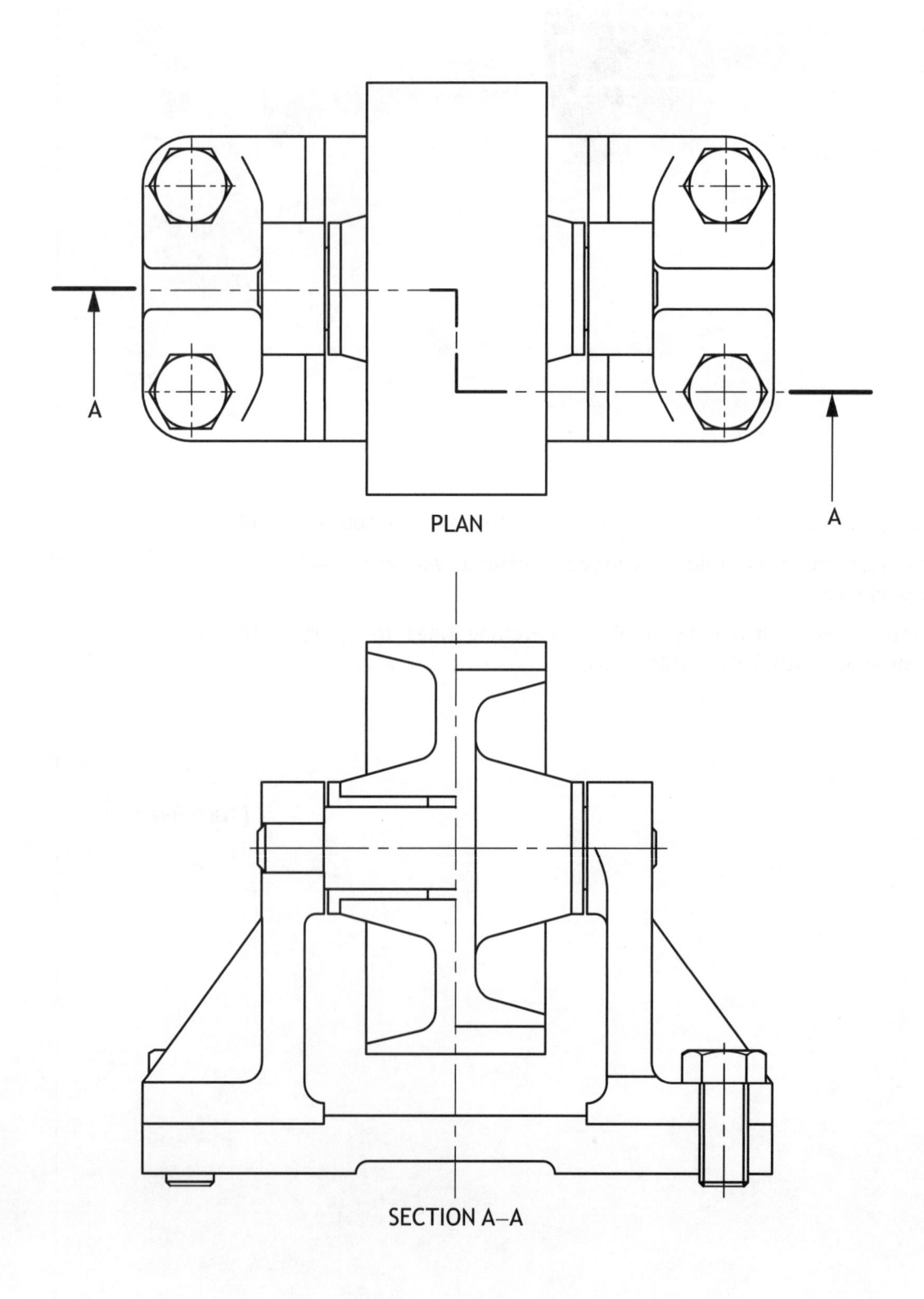

PLAN

SECTION A–A

5. A building company is planning a new residential area. The plan shown below has been illustrated for potential customers. It does not use British Standard conventions.

Houses 19 to 25 are elevated above others on higher ground.

(a) Identify **three** features of **this drawing** which should be shown on a **British Standards** location plan.

3

_____

_____

_____

[Turn over

5. (continued)

   (b) A 3D model of one of the house styles is shown below.

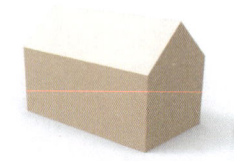

   State the total number of houses of this style in the location plan. 1

   _____

   (c) The architect used the following symbols in the floor plan drawings. State the correct name for each of the symbols. 3

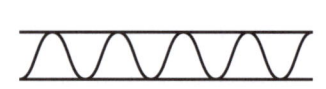

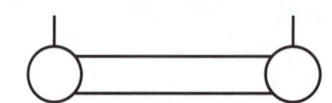

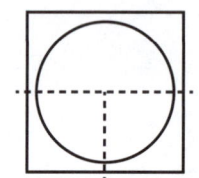

   (i) _____ (ii) _____ (iii) _____

6. A CAD technician created a 3D model of the fire extinguisher, shown below.

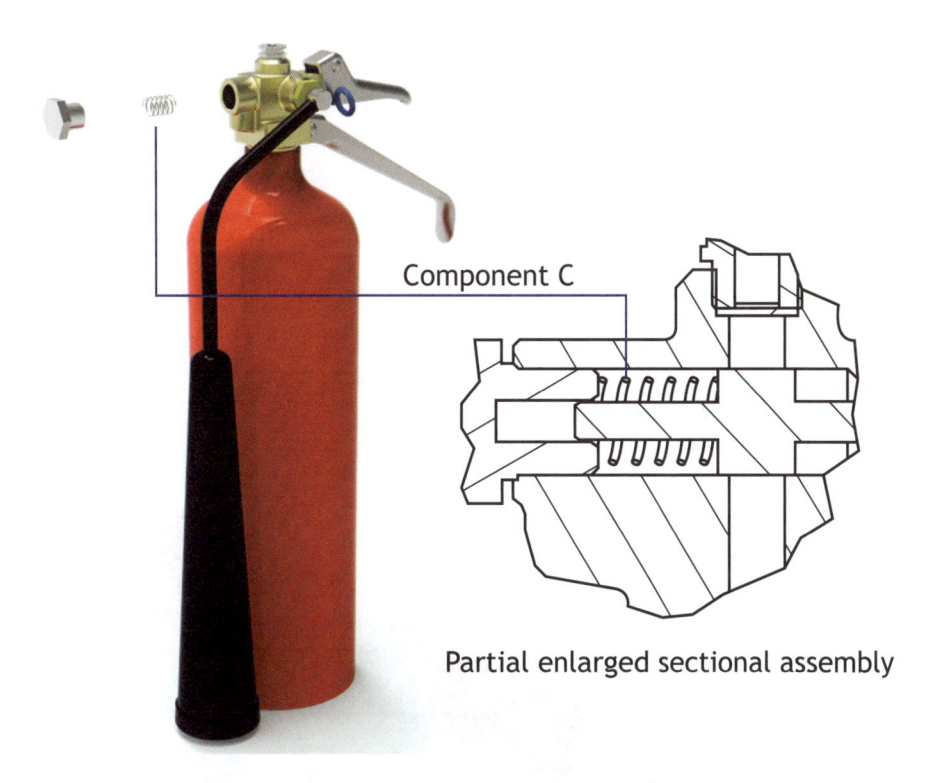

Component C

Partial enlarged sectional assembly

(a) Describe the 3D CAD modelling technique used to create component C. You may use sketches to illustrate your answer.

2

6. (continued)

Look at the drawing of the pipe and nozzle sub-assembly shown below. The CAD technician used this to create models of the individual components.

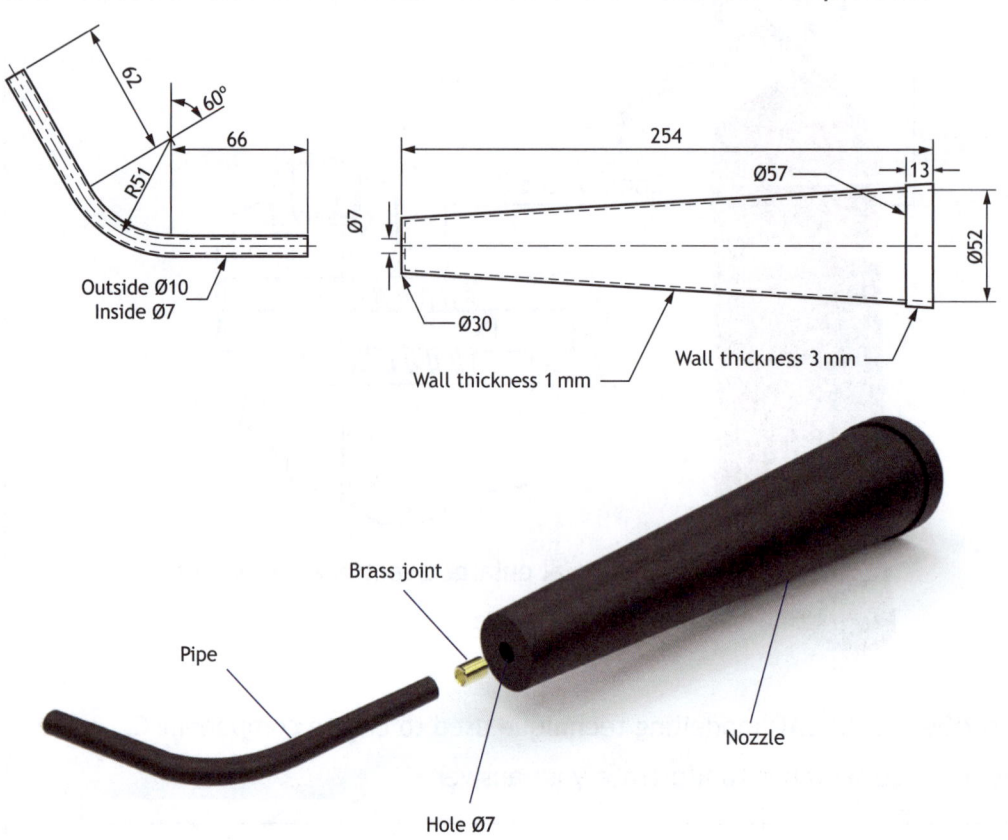

(b) Describe the 3D CAD modelling techniques used to create the **pipe** component.

You must refer to the dimensions given in the drawing.

3

6. (continued)

The manufacturer of the fire extinguisher would like to provide a simple wall bracket to hold their product.

Pictorial

Hook hole

Ø10
Ø114
30

Plan

10
376

End elevation

Elevation

Centre of pin 32 mm from wall face

62

Notes to the CAD technician

Must fit hook hole on fire extinguisher

Screw holes to attach to wall: must have four holes.

Wall thickness is 10 mm

Small recess to fit the bottom of the fire extinguisher 5 mm deep.

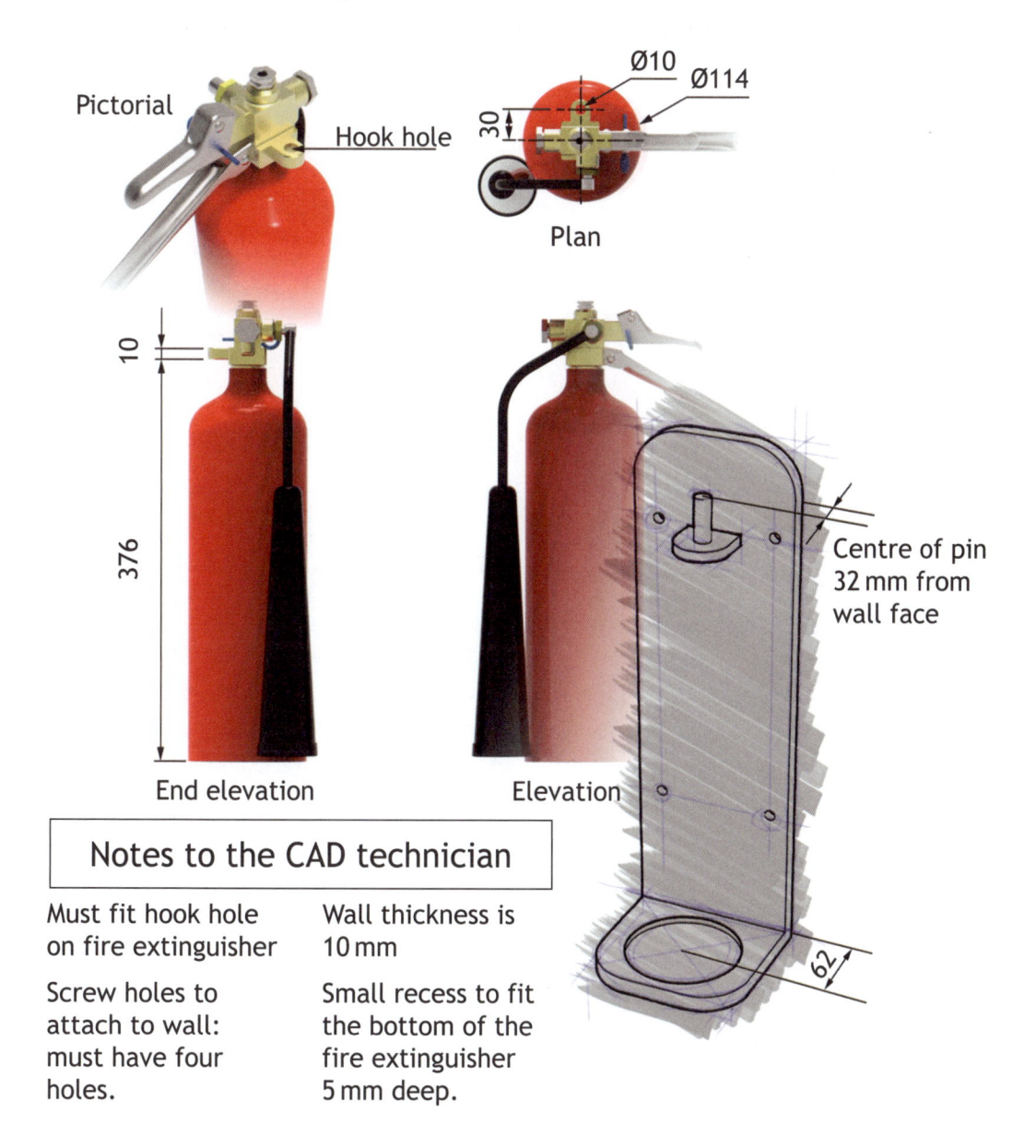

[Turn over

6. (continued)

(c) Describe the 3D CAD modelling techniques used to create the wall bracket.

Use measurements from the rendered orthographic and the notes to the CAD technician.

You may use sketches to illustrate your answer.

7

MARKS

7. Glasgow Riverside Museum opened in 2011. The architect firm was required to submit a number of drawings to the local authority to gain planning permission. During this process the architects also produced a number of other graphics for different purposes.

Figure 1

Figure 2

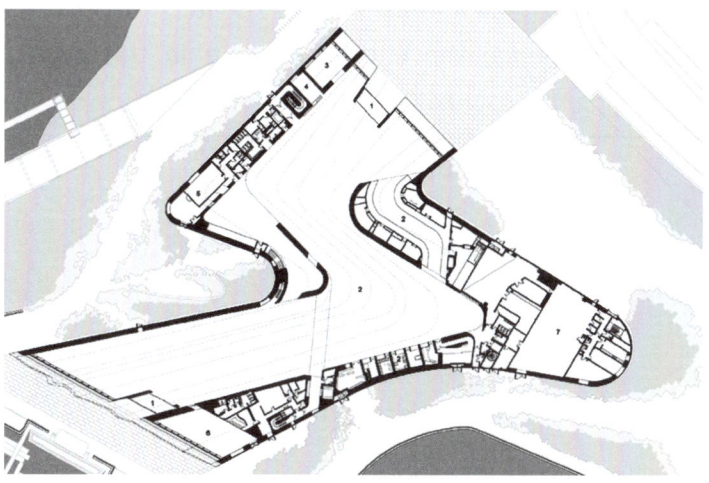

Figure 3

Page twenty-five [Turn over

7. (continued)

   (a) **Explain**, with reference to the 3Ps, the purpose of each of the graphics shown in Figures 1, 2 and 3. **3**

   (b) The scales commonly used for Figure 3 are 1:50 or 1:100.

   State **two** factors that influence the choice of scale in this type of graphic. **2**

7. (continued)

Sectional views are commonly used in the construction industry.
Cross-hatching is a feature found in sectional construction views.

(c) Describe two benefits of applying cross-hatching to a sectional construction drawing. 2

[END OF SPECIMEN QUESTION PAPER]

ADDITIONAL SPACE FOR ANSWERS

ADDITIONAL SPACE FOR ANSWERS

[BLANK PAGE]

DO NOT WRITE ON THIS PAGE

HIGHER
Answers

ANSWERS FOR

SQA HIGHER GRAPHIC COMMUNICATION 2018

General Marking Principles for Higher Graphic Communication

Questions that ask candidates to "describe"

Candidates must provide a statement or structure of characteristics and/or features. This should be more than an outline or a list. Candidates may refer to, for instance, a concept, experiment, situation, or facts in the context of and appropriate to the question. The number of marks available for a question indicates the number of factual/appropriate points required.

Questions that ask candidates to "explain"

Candidates must generally relate cause and effect and/or make relationships between things clear. These will be related to the context of the question or a specific area within a question.

Questions that ask candidates to "compare"

Candidates must generally demonstrate knowledge and understanding of the similarities and/or differences between, for instance, things, methods, or choices. These will be related to the context of the question or a specific area within a question.

Candidates can respond to any question using text, sketching, annotations or combinations where they prefer. No marks shall be awarded for the quality of sketching. Marking will relate only to the information being conveyed.

HIGHER GRAPHIC COMUNICATION 2017

Question			Expected response	Max mark
1.	(a)	(i)	• Can generate production drawings and assembly information to assist manufacture • Can generate drawings with dimensions • 3D models can be directly used for manufacture • 3D models allow manufacturers to evaluate sizes or design features, colours and materials prior to manufacture	2
		(ii)	Allows testing of: • Moving parts • Strength of parts • How parts fit together • Weight/mass of parts and/or assemblies • Centre of mass • Strength of materials	2
	(b)		Radial array	1

Question		Expected response	Max mark
	(c)	• Diameter/radius of profile from axis @ 40 mm (1 mark) • Axis @ 320 mm or 8 revolutions of profile (1 mark) • Feature as a helix (1 mark)	3
	(d)	• Describe or sketch the profile and path (1 mark) • Extrude along a path/Sweep along a path (1 mark)	2
	(e)	• Top down modelling ensures the component will fit the handlebar without having to specify any dimensions • The rubber handles will be modelled in situ and not need assembly constraints • Any change in the handle bars will dynamically change the handles	2
	(f)	**Revolve method** • The grip length dimensions 5,5 and 120 mm (1 mark) • Internal and external diameter of 20 and 28 mm (1 mark) • Diameter of hand-stop 52 mm (1 mark) • Grip dimensions 1 × 1 mm square 5 mm from top surface (1 mark) • Linear array of grip profile 38 times, gap 2 mm (1 mark) • Revolve profile (1 mark) **Extrusion method** • 3 extrusions dia 28 up 5 mm, dia 52 up 5 mm and dia 28 up 120 mm (1 mark) • Extrude-subtract dia 20 mm cylinder 130 mm to create hollow feature (1 mark) • Create 2D sketch on a workplane perpendicular and through centre axis of feature (1 mark) • Create sketch of 1 mm square 5 mm from top surface (1 mark) • Revolve-subtract sketch (1 mark) • Linear array this feature 38 times, gap 2 mm (1 mark)	6
	(g) (i)	Removed section	1
	(ii)	Revolved section	1

ANSWERS FOR HIGHER GRAPHIC COMMUNICATION

Question			Expected response	Max mark
2.	(a)	(i)	Explanations should make appropriate reference to: **Graphic 1** User: • Potential buyer • Client • Investor • Interior Designer • Any other relevant answer Purpose: • Promotional type graphic • Show colour, textures, materials • Shows internal building layout • Has furniture in place • Any other relevant answer	2
		(ii)	**Graphic 2** User: • Construction industry • Builder • Joiner • Planning department • Architect • Any other relevant answer Purpose: • Includes technical details that would allow construction • Contains dimensions • Shows building materials • Any other relevant answer	2
	(b)	(i)	Responses should include: • Ease of collaboration within company • Potentially available on demand anywhere • Many staff can collaborate simultaneously • Can be accessed remotely • Use with mobile devices	2
		(ii)	Responses should include: • Cloud could be hacked • Intellectual property stolen • Digital rights management issues • Requires access to internet at all times • Cloud servers may fail • Virus infection of the system/software	2
3.	(a)	(i)	• Using lines above and below the pull quote • Making the pull quote a different colour from the body text • Centre justification of the text • Placing the pull quote out with the grid structure • Using a different typeface or font	1
		(ii)	Adding a drop cap	1
		(iii)	• Making it the largest item in the layout • It is a cropped image • It is a close-up image	1

	(b)		• It creates a less busy looking (calming) layout • It creates harmony in the layout • No single colour dominates the layout • Advancing, warm colours relates to the article • Limited colours in the layout makes the large graphic stand out	2
	(c)		• To create contrast between the typefaces • To create visual interest	1
	(d)		• It is a light, elegant font and will appeal to the target audience • It is a more formal or traditional style that reflects the theme of the article	1
	(e)		• Repetition of circular shape • Colour matching creates rhythm • Use of bullet points	1
	(f)		• Background texture	1
	(g)		• Circles decrease in value (increasing the tint/saturation of the colour) • Images have low value creating contrast with the background	1
4.	(a)	(i) to (iv)	**Feature:** Drop cap **Reasons:** • The drop cap draws the reader's eye to the beginning of the main body text • The colour red helps create unity with other similar colours in the layout, tying various elements together in a subtle way • The colour red creates strong visual contrast with the white background. **OR** **Feature:** Column rule or Gutter **Reasons:** • The column rule makes the main body text easier to read as it separates both columns clearly • The designer has also adjusted the gutter width to accommodate the column rule and improve legibility • Vertical column rule creates contrast with horizontal red rule	

ANSWERS FOR HIGHER GRAPHIC COMMUNICATION

Question			Expected response	Max mark
			OR **Feature:** Sub heading or emboldened text	1
			Reasons: <ul><li>The sub-heading allows the reader to get a brief overview of the article without having to read though the main body text</li><li>The bold typeface draws the reader's eye to the subheading</li><li>The bold typeface contrasts with the body text below</li></ul>	2
			OR **Feature:** Pull quote or text box (with colour fill)	1
			Reasons: Pull quote <ul><li>Gives the reader a quick preview of the content of the article</li><li>Catches the reader's eye</li><li>Creates depth by layering over image and flash-bar</li><li>Unity created with red flash bar behind caption with other red elements on the layout</li></ul>	2
			OR **Feature:** Text box re-size (White)	1
			Reasons: Text box re-size <ul><li>Creates a larger area for text and allows space for the insertion of a pull quote</li><li>Also gives a bigger backdrop for the player graphic</li></ul>	2
	(b)	(i)	An image that contains a large number of pixels per unit area	1
		(ii)	Accept format types Bitmap (BMP), Jpeg (JPG), Portable Network Graphic (PNG) or Tagged Image File Format (TIFF)	1
	(c)		<ul><li>Watermarking is a means of protecting the intellectual property of the company</li><li>It can also act as an advertisement for the company as it contains their logo and brand identity (it can potentially lead to future business)</li><li>To stop others from selling or passing off the images as their own</li><li>Prevents use of image without payment being made</li></ul>	2

Question		Expected response	Max mark
5.	(a)		1
	(b)		6
6.	(a)	■ 1 mark • 1 mark ∗ 1 mark ▲ 1 mark • 1 mark ♥ 1 mark SECTION A–A	6
	(b)	As indicated above	3

HIGHER GRAPHIC COMMUNICATION 2018

Question			Expected response	Max mark
1.	(a)		• Parts are modelled individually • They can be inserted into an assembly to position and fix them in relation to other components • Any changes to a part will need to be done by editing it individually	2
	(b)	(i)	Major axis 126 mm	1
		(ii)	Minor axis 40 mm	1
	(c)		• Sketch/description of profile and extrude 30 mm • Dia 40 mm circle in correct position, extrude 10 mm • Dia 15 mm circle in correct position, extrude subtract material 20 mm • Fillet radius 5 mm, chamfer 5 mm	4
	(d)		• Describe the profile (dia 15 mm circle), describe the path with dimensions shown on elevation **(1 mark)** • Extrude/sweep along a path command **(1 mark)** • Shell 2·5 mm wall thickness **(1 mark)**	3
	(e)		• Profile sketch with all dimensions **(1 mark)** • Describe centre axis **(1 mark)** • Revolve command **(1 mark)** Horizontal 5 mm, 7·5 mm Vertical 7·5 mm, 23 mm 37·5 mm Radius 15 mm	3
	(f)		Ø10·15 / Ø9·75 Ø10 +0·15 / −0·25 TOLERANCE APPLIED TOLERANCE APPLIED 1 mark for correct sizes. 1 mark for correct BS convention.	2
	(g)		• Describe the grip profile, dia 44 × 5 mm, on correct workplane **(1 mark)** • Extrude 20 mm long **(1 mark)** • Radial array command, repeat 12 times **(1 mark)**	3
	(h)	(i)	• Find the radial array command on the modeling tree. Edit/change the value.	1
		(ii)	• It would take longer to redo the whole grip part than to edit the command.	1
2.	(a)	(i)	STEP file *Also acceptable:* • .stp file extension	1
		(ii)	• These files can be opened in any 3D modelling packages • They allow the manufacturer to make edits/changes, if required prior to manufacture	1
	(b)		• Edits can be made to the original graphics • Vector graphics will retain their quality if enlarged • Vector files are smaller in file size	1
	(c)		*Any two from:* • Components can be called from the library rather than drawn from scratch • Quality control, less errors • Components drawn to common standards • Technicians can share CAD library resources	2
	(d)	(i)	3rd angle projection	1
		(ii)	• It allows the company to see the projection method used within the drawing • This will assist with the interpreting of the information given and the view positioning	1
3.	(a)	(i)	Promotional — allows manufacturer to advertise their products/services to potential customers.	1
		(ii)	Production — aids with assembly of the product.	1
	(b)		• Gives an accurate real-life representation • Can be quickly produced showing how products would look in the customer's own home without the need to produce a detailed manual sketch • Designs can be shared electronically without the need to scan • Renders showing different colour/material combinations can be produced instantly • Designs can be easily modified • Templates can be created for multiple designs	2
4.	(a)		16 mm	1
	(b)	(i)	★ 1 mark – Ceiling Fixing Mount ▲ 1 mark – Fixing Cover ● 1 mark – Mounting Bracket ✚ 1 mark – Hatching into thread *1 mark for each correctly sectioned component.*	4

ANSWERS FOR HIGHER GRAPHIC COMMUNICATION

	(ii)	STRAIGHT KNURLING (1 mark) DIAMOND KNURLING (1 mark)	2
	(c) (i)	Pitch Circle Diameter	1
		30 degrees	1
5.	(a)	Justification of repetition of shapes on graphic: • circles/lines in background • white lines dividing columns down middle of page • yellow bars containing headers • double yellow arrows • shape for batteries • white figures.	2
	(b)	• Divides columns into equal sections • Grid creates consistency/visual harmony throughout publication • Helps to guides the reader's eye from column to column • Easier to read the publication	2
	(c)	• Repetition of colour yellow throughout publication • Repetition of blue text • Repetition of white text and graphics • Repetition of same font/typeface throughout publication • Use of white line for 'cable' tightly wrapping around columns, creates unity through close proximity • Repeated use of 'silhouette' figures • Repetition of white drop caps	2
	(d)	• Drop shadow behind 'Energy Bill' gives impression of depth • The background layer creates impression of depth • Value of background creates depth	2
	(e)	• Alignment of text • Alignment of line • Alignment of shape • Alignment of vertical lines on 'cable' • Alignment of battery symbol	2
	(f)	• Use of drop cap at the start of each paragraph • Enlarged text for 'Energy Bill' creates emphasis • Drop shadow on 'Energy Bill' • Blue text on yellow flash bar	2

6.	(a)	Response must be in relation to the consumer. • Allows instant access to hyperlinks/websites that the publication is talking about • Multiple publications can be stored on an electronic device and referenced to at any time without cluttering up a home/office • When viewing, the information can be enlarged for better clarity or closer inspection, change size of text • Can be shared across a number of devices for the owner • Sharing elements/videos/images on social media or email • Can copy and paste content • No need to visit shop or wait for it to be delivered • Can be read in the dark • Available in different languages • Online content can have the most 'up to date' information	2
	(b)	Response must be in relation to the company. • Better business opportunities for the company with different countries • More people can access and understand the written information on the website	1
	(c)	• Clarity and readability • Physical size of device will determine size of text being viewed • Typeface may reflect style of magazine/target market	2
	(d)	• Serif font — the letters have decorative strokes on the ends of the characters. ## Serif *Also acceptable:* • A sketch	1
	(e)	• Information can be accessed regardless of location • Can be accessed and shared with all the web designers • Can be accessed on multiple devices or platforms • Information can be downloaded/uploaded at any time • Portable devices with less storage capacity can access the information as items will be saved in the cloud, not the device	2

ANSWERS FOR HIGHER GRAPHIC COMMUNICATION

	(f)	(i)	• Used on the main body text rectangle. Allows the graphic to be seen and the text still to be read	1
		(ii)	• Description of orange colour matched elements creating unity in the document	1
	(g)		• The contrast in text size creates emphasis • To lead the readers eye to the start of a paragraph/section of text	2
	(h)		Identification **1 mark** • Title 'Bright Spark' • Company logo of Eiffel Tower • Company name Paris • Text on R-H side of DTP document • QR codes Effect **1 mark** • Creates contrast with black background • Adds emphasis to company name and logo • Catches the eye of the reader	2
6.	(i)		• Centre justified text used on R-H side of page, fits with the centre alignment of graphics on this side • Fully justified text on main body text, give clear straight edges that suit the rectangle shape it is placed within, adds structure and formality to the page • Creates contrast between the two types of justification	1
	(j)		• Used to separate areas of the magazine page • Creates unity with the orange colour • Creates contrast in shape with the wavy flame lines in the background • Creates contrast with the horizontal flashbar at the bottom of the page	2

HIGHER GRAPHIC COMMUNICATION 2018 SPECIMEN QUESTION PAPER

Question			Expected response	Max mark
1.	(a)		• Reduce time required to model each component • Reduce likelihood of CAD technician making errors • Represents actual standard component parts • A library would contain all common component parts • The same parts would be used by all CAD technicians in the company • Library components can be used by CAD users worldwide	2
	(b)	(i)	• Gives a realistic representation of what the final product will look like • 3D models can be used to create photorealistic renders • 3D models can be used to show different materials, colours and textures • 3D models can be animated • 3D models can be put into different scenes or contexts • Used for promotional material (print or digital)	1
		(ii)	• 3D models can be used to directly manufacture (CNC/CAM) • To enable dimensions to be extracted from the CAD model, without production drawings • 3D models can be used to show how complex items are assembled • 3D models do not need a manufacturer to interpret complex production drawings • Production drawings can be created and fully dimensioned from the CAD model	1
	(c)		• Top down modelling allows sizes to be captured from another part, without measuring • Top down modelling allows geometry (form and shape) to be captured without redrawing • Top down modelling ensures the 3D CAD model is automatically assembled • Top down modelling allows the change of one component to automatically update another component • Components can be created in context within an assembly	2
	(d)	(i)	Use 'Offset' command	1
		(ii)	Select the bottom edge of the guitar and set a distance	1

ANSWERS FOR HIGHER GRAPHIC COMMUNICATION

Question			Expected response	Max mark
	(e)		**Revolve method** • Using the revolve command (1 mark) • Describing the profile to be revolved, with dimensions (1 mark) • Creating a circle on a perpendicular plane and extrude subtract (1 mark) • Describing the dimensioning of circle diameter 4 mm on the perpendicular workplane and its position 9 mm up from the base (1 mark) • Creating diameter 5 mm circle on the base, extrude subtract to 11 mm depth (1 mark) Award 1 mark where candidate has added this feature in the revolve. Creating ridges: **Extrude along a path method** • Creating a circle for ridge on top face (1 mark) • Creating a sketch-path to correct length, extrude-along-a-path (subtract) (1 mark) • Radial array ridge feature 38 times over PCD 14 (1 mark) **Loft Method** • Using the loft command (1 mark) • Describing relevant dimensions, 3 offset distances for 4 workplanes (1 mark) • Creating a circle on a perpendicular plane and extrude subtract (1 mark) • Describing the dimensioning of circle diameter 4 mm on the perpendicular workplane and its position 9 mm up from the base (1 mark) • Creating diameter 5 mm circle on the base, extrude subtract to 11 mm depth (1 mark) Creating ridges: **Loft method** • Creating a circle for ridge on top face (1 mark) • Creating bottom circle and loft between profiles (subtract) (1 mark)	8

Question			Expected response	Max mark
			• Radial array ridge feature 38 times over PCD 14 (1 mark)	
	(f)	(i)	Correct symbol in correct position (1 mark)	1
		(ii)	Correct symbol in correct position (1 mark)	1
	(g)	(i)	90 mm	1
		(ii)	12 mm	1
	(h)		• Describing using loft command (1 mark) • Describing workplanes offset (1 mark) • Describing profiles (1 mark)	3
2.	(a)	(i)	• Area of white space underneath FAB emphasises the heading and attracts the eye to it • Area of white space bleeds from left page onto the right • Area of white space creates breathing space/a rest for the eye • Areas of white space make the page look less cluttered Triangular white space creates • Balance • Interest • Rhythm	2
		(ii)	• Warm colour yellow is used that has connotations of summer and warmth • Harmonious colour scheme • The repeated use of the colour yellow creates unity in the layout • Contrast in colours on sunglasses — blue and yellow	2
		(iii)	• Sans serif font used for FAB title. Its simplicity works well with the image behind it • The layout has a combination of serif and sans serif and script fonts creating a stylised feel — reflecting the target market • Contrasting fonts in the layout create visual interest	2

Question		Expected response	Max mark
(b)		• Emphasis created by enlarged heading being larger than all other elements • Triangular images very similar in size, helping to create unity/consistency — also means that no image is more dominant than the other • Areas of body text are similar in size which helps create consistency and balance • Enlarged cropped images within triangular frames create visual interest	4
(c)		• Pictorial/perspective view of the sunglasses themselves gives the illusion of depth against the flat background • Drop shadow on Ray-Ban logo yellow background • Drop shadow on sunglasses image • Drop shadow on bottom yellow box • Image behind FAB transparency gives depth • Transparency added to top-left image creates illusion of depth • Different sizes of figures in images creates depth	2
(d)		• The yellow colour of the line creates unity with other yellow elements on the page • The line draws the reader's eye from left to right and around the image • The stroke/thickness of the line is consistent and narrow, meaning it is not overpowering/dominant • Angle of lines creates interest/shape on the page • Lines are used to emphasise the triangular image and the triangular white space • Lines separate/split elements on the page	2
(e)		• Scalable without pixelation • The red background could be easily changed to yellow within the DTP software. Had the image been a bitmap it would have to have been edited using specialist software • The white text can be made transparent within the DTP software • The red background could be stretched easily within the DTP software without the need for prior editing in another package	2

Question		Expected response	Max mark
(f)		• Text and images can be edited separately • Layers can be turned on and off to improve clarity during the production of the layout • The mask for FAB could be easily created • The layers can provide a master page for similar future layouts • Edit layers without affecting other parts of the layout • Layers can be reordered, moved to front, moved to back	3
(g)	(i)	Centred justification for all the text on the left-hand page creates balance and/or symmetry or alignment or contrast	1
	(ii)	Fully justified text provides neatness as there are no jagged edges on the sides of columns	1
(h)	(i)	No white spaces will appear outside the yellow boxes after cropping	1
	(ii)	• To allow the multicolour printing to be set up correctly • Each register mark should overprint exactly for accurate registration	2
3.	(a)	Answer should summarise points that include the following. **CAD location plans show** • Location of building in relation to streets • Location of building in relation to other buildings • Size of building to scale • Contours show the slope in the land • Geographical features, eg rivers, woodland, greenbelt • Position of existing railways, bridges • North symbol will show the direction the building is facing **CAD site plans show** • Proposed building in relation to the property boundaries • Size and position of the building • Position of drainage • Landscape elements • Gas, electrical and water supplies • Contours show the slope in the land • Trees shown in position • North symbol will show the direction the building is facing • Size of the building and site to scale	4

Question			Expected response	Max mark
	(b)		• Photo real image of how the building will look • Realistic representation of materials • Adjacent buildings shown • Building is shown in its proposed environment • Shows adjacent roads and direction of traffic flow • Realistic representations of different lighting conditions in day time, night time • Useful for users who cannot read or interpret 2D drawings such as floor plans, site plans and location plans • Rendered CAD pictorials can be sent out to the community by email	3
	(c)	(i)	The sketches would have to be captured/scanned using a suitable device (flatbed, hand, photocopier used as a scanner, digital camera, digitiser/graphics tablet)	1
		(ii)	• Jpeg files are compressed • Jpeg files are a small size • Jpeg is a common file type • Jpegs are easily accessible without any specialist software	2
	(d)		• The sketches could include realistic material representations • They can be built up in a series of layers to ease editing • They are automatically stored electronically and do not require scanning to upload to the website • Able to show client any changes instantly • Sketches can be exported into other packages • Easy to share via email	2
4.			1 mark for each correctly sectioned component (5 in total) ▲ 1 mark Pulley ★ 1 mark Bush ● 1 mark Left bracket ■ 1 mark Base ● 1 mark Right bracket SECTION A-A	5

Question			Expected response	Max mark
5.	(a)		• Symbols for existing trees OR proposed trees OR trees to be removed OR trees • North symbol • Contour lines • Boundary lines	3
	(b)		Four	1
	(c)	(i)	Insulated board/Insulation board	1
		(ii)	Towel rail	1
		(iii)	Drainage	1
6.	(a)		**Helix** • Describing a **profile** and **axis** (1 mark) • Describing feature command as **helix** (1 mark)	2
	(b)		**Pipe** • Describing **path,** with all **dimensions** (1 mark) • Describing **profile** with OD10 and ID7 (1 mark) • Feature command as **extrude along a path** (1 mark)	3
	(c)		**Wall bracket** • Extruding L-shape bracket (1 mark) • Wall thickness of bracket is 10mm (1 mark) • Circular recess profile is between DIA114mm and 120mm and extrude (subtract) circular recess 5mm deep (1 mark) • Ensuring centre of hook is 32mm from the back of the wall bracket and positioned vertically (1 mark) • Ensuring hook is equal to or less than DIA10mm (1 mark) • Applying four screw holes to bracket (1 mark) • Height from bottom of recess to the bottom of the pin, size 376mm (1 mark)	7

Question			Expected response	Max mark
7.	(a)		**3Ps** Figure 1 — **Promotional graphic** • Realistic rendering of the building • Shows how the completed building will fit in with its environment • Promotion or advertising for the building Figure 2 — **Preliminary graphic** • Gives a sense of scale and form • No specific construction information can be gained • Used to give a sense of how the concept may look Figure 3 — **Production graphic** • Shows how the building will be laid out • Gives details of internal partitions and accommodation	3
	(b)		**Scale** • Size of item • Size of paper • Degree of detail required	3
	(c)		**Cross hatching** • Describe different materials • Describe different components • Show parts that have been cut by the cutting plane	2